CULTURE SMART!

SLOVAKIA

Brendan F. R. Edwards

·K·U·P·E·R·A·R·D·

ISBN 978 1 85733 566 8
This book is also available as an e-book: eISBN 978 1 85733 567 5

British Library Cataloguing in Publication Data
A CIP catalogue entry for this book is available from the British Library

First published in Great Britain
by Kuperard, an imprint of Bravo Ltd
59 Hutton Grove, London N12 8DS
Tel: +44 (0) 20 8446 2440 Fax: +44 (0) 20 8446 2441
www.culturesmart.co.uk
Inquiries: sales@kuperard.co.uk

Series Editor Geoffrey Chesler
Design Bobby Birchall

Printed in India

About the Author

BRENDAN F. R. EDWARDS, M.A., M.L.I.S., Ph.D., is a Canadian academic and writer. He has spent every summer teaching in Slovakia since 2003, and in 2005–6 lived in the Slovak city of Trnava, where he taught English to high school, university, and private students. He has also lived and worked in Romania, and collaborated on several texts on Slovakia and Central Europe, including *Pictoria: The Early History of Slovakia in Images* by Pavel Dvořák (2006), and *Migrating Memories: Central Europeans in Canada* (2 vols., Central European Association for Canadian Studies, 2010). He is the author of several scholarly articles relating to Canada and Slovakia, as well as *Paper Talk: A History of Libraries, Print Culture, and Aboriginal Peoples in Canada before 1960* (Scarecrow Press, 2005).

contents

contents

Map of Slovakia

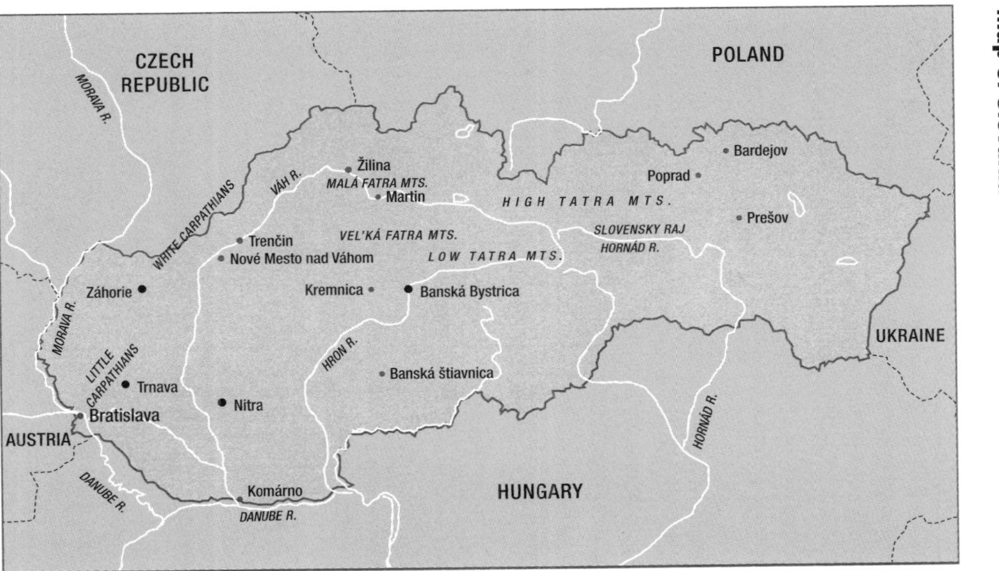

introduction

For most North Americans and Western Europeans, there is little or no distinction between Czechs and Slovaks. Many, in fact, continue to refer to "Czechoslovakia" as though it still existed. Although it is true that for much of the twentieth century Czechs and Slovaks lived together in a single state, their languages are quite similar, and many have intermarried, there are important differences between them. These differences, in part, explain the "Velvet Divorce" of 1993 and the rebirth of a sovereign Slovak state, separate from the Czechs. This book aims to introduce you to the Slovaks' unique cultural characteristics, and to equip you with enough human information to get the very best out of your visit.

Generally speaking, the Slovaks are "more Slavic" than the Czechs—their pace of life is somewhat slower, and their spare time is more often filled with friends, family, and music. Since 1993, the Czech Republic has blossomed. Slovakia, on the other hand, initially struggled as a sovereign state, with an insular government and a low international profile. But in 2004 Slovakia joined the European Union alongside the Czech Republic. Now that it has EU membership and a relatively healthy industrial economy, Europeans are starting to take notice. In recent years Slovakia has demonstrated a confidence all its own. Even though it has been largely overlooked as the Czech Republic's "little sister," Slovakia has much to offer and has been referred to as the economic "tiger" of Europe.

The Slovaks are thought to be resistant to change, if not inflexible, and many Slovaks, when asked, confirm this to be true. Yet the Slovak people have witnessed many changes in the last twenty years—the fall of communism in the "Velvet Revolution" of 1989 and the "Velvet Divorce" of 1993, widespread economic diversification, expansion, and global influence, EU membership in 2004, and the adoption of the Euro in 2009. Change has been a constant in this young state's short economic and political history, and the Slovaks have adapted to it with quiet optimism and a modest sense of pride.

As members of a small nation with a short political history—but an old culture—Slovaks respond readily to foreigners who are aware of their separate identity, master a few words of Slovak, and show an interest in their traditions. Firmly Central European (as opposed to Eastern European, which was largely a construct of the Cold War), they call their country "the heart of Europe"—a term applicable not only in geographic terms, but also in describing the Slovak character, which is warm, deeply hospitable, and immensely proud. And while Slovakia is not without its frustrations for foreigners, few visitors leave without a positive impression of "the little big country."

Culture Smart! Slovakia describes what makes this country unique, and explains some of the quirks, pitfalls, and memorable aspects of Slovak life. Of course, generalization has its limitations, and there may well be exceptions to the advice and situations described here, but with this guide in hand, and an open mind, you will be well positioned to make the most of your Slovak travels and experiences.

Key Facts

Official Name	Slovakia (Slovensko) or Slovak Republic (Slovenská Republika)	Born of the "Velvet Divorce" from the Czech Republic in 1993; member of the EU since 2004
Capital City	Bratislava	Pop. 429,000 (approx.)
Major Cities	Košice, Trnava, Nitra, Banská Bystrica, Prešov, Trenčín, Žilina	
Area	18,932 sq. miles (49,035 sq. km)	
Borders	Austria, Czech Republic, Poland, Ukraine, Hungary	Longest border with Hungary; entered Schengen border-free zone in 2007
Climate	Between temperate and continental, with generally warm summers and cold, cloudy, humid winters	July temperature average high 79°F (26°C); January average low 19°F (-7°C)
Currency	Euro (€); previously Slovak koruna (SKK)	Slovakia entered the euro zone on January 1, 2009.
Population	5,470,306 (July 2010 est.)	Approx. 48.5% men, 51.5% women
Ethnic Makeup	Slovak 85.8%, Hungarian 9.7%, Roma 1.7% (officially, but unofficial estimates place the Roma population as high as 10%), Ruthenian/Ukrainian 1%, other and unspecified 1.8% (2001 census)	
Language	Slovak (official) 83.9%, Hungarian 10.7%, Roma 1.8%, Ukrainian 1%, other and unspecified 2.6% (2001 census)	
Religion	Catholic 68.9%, Protestant 10.8%, Greek Catholic 4.1%, other and unspecified 3.2%, none 13% (2001 census)	

Government	Parliamentary democracy. Head of state is the president; head of government is the prime minister. The president is elected for a five-year term (eligible for a second term).	Cabinet appointed by president on recommendation of prime minister. After elections the leader of the majority party, or coalition, is appointed prime minister by the president.
Media	State TV, Slovenská Televízia, broadcasts on three channels: Jednotka ("One"), Dvojka ("Two"), and Trojka ("Three"), an all-sports channel. Commercial TV companies include Markíza, TV JOJ, and TA3 (all-news).	Slovenský Rozhlas (Slovak Radio), the national public-service radio, broadcasts six radio channels and two digital channels. Commercial radio stations include FUN Rádio and Rádio Expres.
Press	Weekly and daily newspapers include *SME*, *Pravda*, and *Nový čas.*	The *Slovak Spectator* (a weekly published by *SME*) is the only English-lang. newspaper.
Electricity	230 volts, 50 Hz	Rounded two-prong plugs. British appliances require an adaptor; North Americans may need a converter.
Video/TV	PAL format	Region 2 DVDs
Internet Domain	.sk	
Telephone	Slovakia's country code is 421.	To dial out, dial 00 and country code.
Time Zone	GMT/UTC +1	Slovakia has daylight saving time.

chapter **one**

LAND & PEOPLE

". . . tried and tested, but never broken over long centuries of adversity; humble and simple people, clever, bound to their land and traditions, as expressed in their poetry, their music, and the colors of a rich folklore; a people as hard and tenacious as their Tatra Mountains, as serene and optimistic as the green expanse of their valleys and forests; a people, above all, deeply attached to the values of their European civilization: honesty, hard work, family and religious faith, as witnessed by so many popular shrines and stupendous churches."

Archbishop Giovanni Cappa, Vatican ambassador to Slovakia, January 1993

GEOGRAPHICAL SNAPSHOT

Slovaks refer to their country as "the heart of Europe." Many outsiders, however, particularly Westerners, still refer to it as part of "Eastern Europe," due to its forty years behind the Iron Curtain. Today's visitors are advised to adjust their language and thinking when it comes to such terms and assumptions. Bratislava, the captal, is a mere forty miles (64 km) from Vienna, which is certainly considered to be in Western Europe. This makes these two cities the closest capitals in Europe, if we exclude the Vatican City and Rome, and the second-closest in the world, after Kinshasa (Democratic Republic of Congo) and Brazzaville (Republic of Congo). Thus, the preferred term is "Central

Europe," which is geographically correct and also less weighted with the old political and cultural assumptions.

Bordered by the Czech Republic to the northwest, Poland to the north, Ukraine to the east, Hungary to the south, and Austria to the southwest, Slovakia has some remarkable geographical features. Although small in area (18,932 sq. miles, or 49,035 sq. km), it offers mountains, forests, natural spas, three hundred ancient castles and ruins, six hundred caves, national parks, meadows, plains, fields, chasms, canyons, gorges, plateaus, and waterfalls. The country's longest river, the Váh (269 miles, or 433 km), joins the Danube at Komárno. Few other countries in the world offer such a varied landscape in such a small area.

The greatest tourist sites are the mountain ranges, the two most renowned being the High Tatras (Vysoké Tatry) in the north, along the Polish border, and the Low Tatras (Nízke Tatry) in central and eastern Slovakia. Gerlachovský Štít, in the High Tatras, at 8,707 feet (2,655 m), is the highest peak. Two smaller ranges also form the Tatras: the Malá Fatra (Small Fatra) and the Veľká Fatra (Big Fatra). Slovak Paradise (Slovenský Raj), an area of remarkable natural beauty and rare flora and fauna, is also popular with outdoor enthusiasts.

CLIMATE AND WEATHER

A landlocked country, Slovakia has a climate that lies between temperate and continental zones, with relatively hot summers and cold, cloudy, humid winters. More specifically, the country can be divided into three basic climatic zones: the lowlands, the basin, and the mountains.

ANNUAL TEMPERATURES
Lowlands: Bratislava and Košice regions
Average approx. 46 to 50°F (8 to 10°C)
Hottest month (July) approx. 68°F (19 to 20°C)
Coldest month (January) approx. 27°F (-3°C)
Basin: Poprad and Sliač regions
Average approx. 41 to 47°F (5° to 8.5°C)
Hottest month (July) approx. 59 to 65°F (15 to 18.5°C)
Coldest month (January) approx. 21 to 27°F (-6 to -3°C)
Mountains: Orava and Spiš regions
Average less than 41°F (5°C)
Hottest month (July) less than 59°F (15°C)
Coldest month (January) less than 23°F (-5°C)

The highest temperature recorded to date in Slovakia occurred at Hurbanovo, in the lowlands region, on July 20, 2007 (104.5°F or 40.3°C). The lowest temperature to date occurred on February 11, 1929, at Vígľaš-Pstruša in the mountain region (-41.8° F or -41°C). Winter varies slightly in length in the different regions of the country, running from mid-December to mid-February in the lowlands; from late November to mid-March in the basin; and from early November to late May in the mountain region.

The average yearly rainfall ranges from 20.47 inches (520 mm) in the lowlands to 78.74 inches (2,000 mm) in the mountain region.

About 40.8 percent of Slovakia's territory is covered by

forests, located largely in the mountainous areas, whereas 50 percent is covered by agricultural land. During the twentieth century many species-rich meadows and pastures were converted into intensively managed grasslands, which reduced species diversity. Vineyards, gardens, and orchards cover small areas distributed throughout the country; these are important for the preservation of genetic diversity and cultivated plant species. There is a small rain forest close to Sliač and Banská Bystrica.

Endangered habitats are mainly the country's aquatic and wetland ecosystems, as a result of drainage, dams, agricultural runoff, and industrial pollution. As of 2001, 22.1 percent of Slovakia's total land area was protected, and eight mammal species, four birds, and eleven plant species were endangered.

Current environmental issues as far as potential hazards are concerned include air pollution from metallurgical plants, especially in eastern Slovakia, which poses some human health risks, and acid rain. The country sources 35.3 percent of its electricity production from fossil fuels, 47.6 percent from nuclear power, and 17.1 percent from hydropower.

THE REGIONS

Slovakia is divided into eight regions: Bratislava, Trnava, Trenčín, Nitra, Banská Bystrica, Žilina, Košice, and Prešov.

Bratislava and West Slovakia

This region, which includes the major cities of Bratislava, Trnava, Trenčín, and Nitra, is by far the most densely populated and economically strong in the country. It also includes a small area known as Záhorie ("Behind the mountains"—referring to the Little Carpathians, which separate it from the rest of the country) that boasts its own

Slovak dialect, similar to Moravian. Bratislava, the state capital, is naturally the de facto capital of West Slovakia.

West Slovakia—and in particular Bratislava—is noticeably more expensive than other parts of the country. Even by the standards of nearby Vienna, Bratislava will put a dent in your budget. Rents, living expenses, and day-to-day costs in the capital are a source of considerable distress to many Slovaks who work there but cannot afford to live there, instead commuting from nearby towns and cities, such as Trnava. Most locals now tend to avoid even shopping in downtown Bratislava, because the prices tend to be inflated for tourists. They go instead to the large, North American–style shopping centers like Aupark, Shopping Palace, and Eurovea, or the similar but much smaller shopping centers in Trnava, Nitra, and Trenčín.

Banská Bystrica and Middle Slovakia

Middle Slovakia, home in part to Slovakia's most popular recreational site—the Tatra Mountains—is perhaps the most naturally scenic part of the country. Major cities here include Žilina, Martin, and the de facto capital of the region, Banská Bystrica. With extensive forests and a hilly terrain, Middle Slovakia is the least densely settled region in the country. Home to several natural mineral water spas, national parks, and protected areas—including the High and Low Tatras and Slovenský Raj (Slovak Paradise)—much of Middle Slovakia is under some form of environmental protection.

Košice and East Slovakia

East Slovakia, consisting of the official political regions of Prešov and Košice, is commonly considered to be the most economically depressed region in the country—but it is also one of the most beautiful. The city of Košice is the second-largest in Slovakia, and acts as the industrial anchor of the east.

Rich in manmade lakes—including the Zemplínska Šírava resort, the Veľká Domaša reservoir, and the Starina reservoir in the Bukovské vrchy (hills)—the northern half of East Slovakia is the most physically spectacular area, but also the poorest.

The southern half is home to the Slovenské Rudohorie Mountains, well known for their ore deposits. There are several popular tourist destinations here, including the ruins of Spiš Castle (one of the biggest in central Europe), the Gombasecká cave complex, and the town of Bardejov, which has one of the best-preserved medieval town squares in Europe. Košice itself, until 1993, rivaled Bratislava in terms of culture, and in 2013 will be the European capital of culture.

LANGUAGE AND IDENTITY

Slovak national consciousness in its present form first truly came about in the late eighteenth century. Although Slovak speakers had existed in the previous decades and centuries, a widespread national awakening was influenced and supported by the debates that emerged in this period around the codification of the Slovak language. Thus, the literature of Slovakia is closely tied to the Slovak sense of national history. Even before these debates, Slovak intellectuals and clerics had been publishing works in Slovakized Czech or a western Slovak vernacular.

A reform in 1786 by the Habsburg monarch Joseph II (Holy Roman Emperor, 1765–90) obliged government officials to explain legislation in the languages of the various peoples of his realm, and this also gave impetus and substance to a Slovak national consciousness. One of Europe's most enlightened despots, Joseph II encouraged education in the vernacular—which in turn encouraged literacy in various Slovak dialects—and issued the Tolerance Patent, legalizing Protestant religions.

These developments, as well as the subsequent influence of the French Revolution (which weakened monarchies throughout Europe and led to a general spread of nationalism), increased the feeling of being culturally limited under Hungarian rule. The time was ripe for what is now referred to as the Slovak National Awakening.

Codification of the language was a challenge not in terms of the exercise itself, but in the choice of Slovak dialect from which a literary language would be created. During the seventeenth and eighteenth centuries there were two competing language areas—central Slovak and western Slovak. Given the importance of Bratislava as a political center, and of Trnava as a cultural and economic center, the first attempt at codifying the language was made on the basis of western Slovak dialects spoken in and around these two cities. The western Slovak dialect was codified by Anton Bernolák (1762–1813), a Catholic priest, between 1784 and 1790. His codified Slovak did not catch on, however, as it did not have enough support from the

intelligentsia outside western Slovakia, from the citizenry who spoke other local dialects, or from the Protestant clergy who used biblical Czech.

Following the failure of early-nineteenth-century efforts to reform Slovakized Czech to better reflect Slovak interests, many Slovaks came to realize that the Czechs were neglecting Slovak concerns. Worse, Magyar nationalism was intensifying, pressuring Slovaks to adopt the Hungarian language and Hungarian names. A common literary language, acceptable and accessible to western, central, and eastern Slovaks, and Catholics and Protestants alike, was necessary to unite all Slovaks.

The linguistic/intellectual leader of this generation was Ľudovít Štúr (1815–56), a Lutheran priest, politician, writer, and thinker. As a historian of the culture of various Slav peoples, Štúr concluded that Slovaks were entitled to their own national culture and language, and that Slovak was not merely a dialect of older Czech, as some had argued. In 1846 he published a treatise defending the need for a Slovak literary language, and a year later he set out the principles for a new

Slovak grammar. Štúr switched from western Slovak to the central Slovak dialect because this dialect enjoyed a considerable prestige as the main vehicle of popular oral culture, and, perhaps more importantly, it was understandable to Slovaks in both east and west. A compromise between Štúr's central literary Slovak and Bernolák's western Slovak version was finally reached in 1851. The new language quickly produced a literary output of considerable quality, thus anchoring it definitively, and leading to a flowering of Slovak literature.

AN UNKNOWN LITERATURE

Unfortunately the literary output that followed the national awakening has been badly neglected by translators, and is thus not generally recognized in the English-speaking world. Simply put, Czech writing has overshadowed Slovak writing. The poets Pavol Országh Hviezdoslav (1849–1921), Svetozár Hurban-Vajanský (1847–1916), and Ivan Krasko (1876–1958) are among the country's best-loved writers. The prose writer Jozef Cíger-Hronský (1896–1961) is one of the few Slovak writers whose work has been translated into English. His novel *Jozef Mak* (1933) is about social conflicts in a Slovak village. Martin M. Šimečka (b. 1957) is one of the few contemporary writers whose work has been translated into English. His *Year of the Frog* (1985) is a fictionalized novel of his experiences as a child of a political dissident. The 1994 collection of short stories *Description of a Struggle* (Picador Press) includes English translations of other contemporary Slovak writers.

A BRIEF HISTORY

Misunderstood, Misinterpreted, and Unknown

Slovak history, like the history of any people, is subject to debate. It is certain, however, that foreign visitors who know nothing of Slovak cultural history—or at least the general history of the Central European region—will be found wanting. The history of migrations and the kingdoms of Central Europe have uniquely shaped modern Slovakia, which has variously been ruled by Hungarians, Austrians, Russians, Czechs, and Germans—and some would now extend this to EU legislation and foreign tourism.

Slovakia's declaration of independence in 1993 was not so much the birth of a new state as the reemergence of a preexisting nation—but a nation about which the outside world knew very little. Slovak history, from a Western historical perspective at least, has been variously described as misunderstood, misinterpreted, and unknown.

At the time when the Slovaks joined the Czechs in their common state in 1918, Slovak history and national aspirations were basically unknown in the West, as there were very few accessible written histories of Slovakia until well into the twentieth century. The Slovaks' sense of themselves until this time had come mainly through song and poetry, and rarely through writing of a scholarly nature. The misunderstanding and misinterpretation of Slovak history was chiefly due to the political and cultural situation that Slovakia found itself in during forty years of communism and to the seemingly deliberate Czech policy simply to label Slovaks as Czechs. This policy was first apparent in the writings and political activities of Czechoslovakia's first president, Tomáš G. Masaryk (1850–1937). At best, twentieth-century writing on Slovakia appeared as hardly more than a postscript to Czech history, or one which for the most part denied the prior existence of a separate Slovak nation and history.

Nonetheless, the seventy-four years between the creation and dissolution of Czechoslovakia were a short period in the history of both peoples, and the Slovaks for one have a past that goes back centuries. The word "Slovakia," as a geographical and political term, appeared for the first time only in 1849, in a petition to the Habsburg Empire. But for the Slovaks, the land north of the Danube and in the Tatras has always been home, even if the geographical and political boundaries of their nation have not always been clear. The Slovak people have always struggled to survive the challenges they have faced as a result of living at the crossroads of Central Europe, and have continually sought to determine their own destiny and make a contribution to European civilization. The Slovak Republic that appeared on the map as of January 1, 1993, covers the territory Slovaks have always inhabited, even if they previously had no formal state to call their own.

The Beginnings of Slovak History

Aside from archaeological remains and artifacts dating from much earlier periods, evidence indicates that the Slavic tribes had widely colonized the area of today's Slovakia by the end of the fifth century AD.

The history of the Slovak people, and thus Slovakia, properly begins with the creation of the Great Moravian Empire in the early ninth century. This state was composed of three Slavic principalities, two of which concern the Slovaks: Morava, which encompassed territory in western Slovakia and modern-day Moravia in the Czech Republic, and Nitra, covering an area in western and central Slovakia, separated by the White Carpathian mountain range. Although it existed for less than three-quarters of a century (833–906), in Slovak oral tradition Great Moravia's existence is the most important event in its short history. In other words, Slovaks remember that they had a state in the ninth century.

Most significantly during the Great Moravian period, two Greek religious scholars and priests, Constantine (Cyril) and Methodius, who had earlier created a basic alphabet for the Slavic language, came to the territory in 863 and brought with them Christianity and literacy. The Cyrillo-Methodian legacy—mainly writing and religion—were important developments, which, alongside geography, helped to secure the historical legacy of Great Moravia as (in part) a Slovak state.

Slovaks and Celts

Modern-day Slovakia is a region where Celts once dwelt. Of the Irish, who are descendants of the Celts, some say that they are "Slovaks who left home early."

Under the Magyars, 896–1918

When the Magyars first laid siege to the Great Moravian state in 896, the Slovaks' brief taste of quasi-statehood disappeared. Fleeing attacks by Bulgarians and Pechenegs (Turks), the Magyars came to the area in search of a homeland, settled down, and created a new state, in which the Slovaks would live until the twentieth century. Significantly, however, in their early relationship with the Hungarians the Slavic tribes were allowed to maintain their languages. Slovak linguists believe that Slovak acquired the status of an independent Slavic language sometime in the tenth or eleventh centuries.

Slovak society within the Hungarian kingdom, until the end of the Middle Ages, at least, was more or less respected, with the Slovak language and nationality being allowed to subsist. But as the Middle Ages drew to a close a long series of invasions into Central Europe by the Ottoman Turks began; a Habsburg ascended the Hungarian throne (in the wake of the Ottoman victory at the Battle of Mohács in 1526); and major threats were posed to Slovak survival.

After the Ottoman victory over the Magyars in 1526, Slovakia (or Royal Hungary—the portion of the Kingdom of Hungary ruled by the Habsburgs) became the center of the Hungarian state. Trnava (Nagyszombat in Hungarian; Tyrnau in German) became the seat of the archbishopric and the Hungarian parliament met in Bratislava (Pozsony to the Hungarians; Pressburg to the Germans), thus making it de facto the capital of Hungary. But whereas Slovak and Hungarian history had until this point been juxtaposed, they henceforth became intertwined.

In addition to being challenged by the Turks, Royal Hungary (Slovakia) and the Habsburgs were threatened by

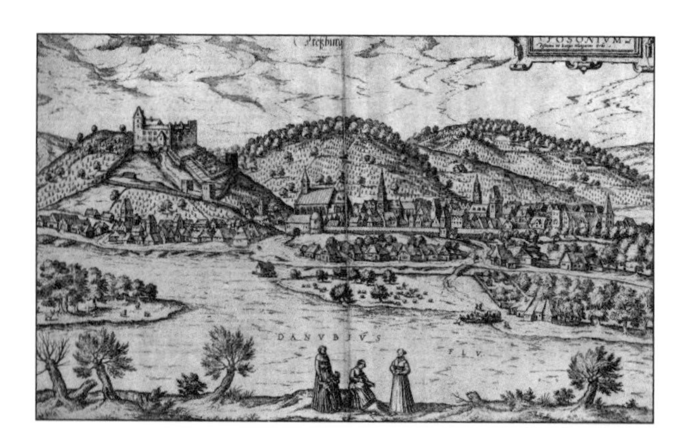

the Protestant Reformation, which initially made deep inroads into Slovakia (where German colonists were especially receptive to its message). With Protestant orders threatening Catholic power in the region, a Counter-Reformation took root, the results of which were vast improvements in education and literacy and an entrenchment of Catholicism among the Slovak population.

The First Czechoslovak State, 1918–38

"Our thousand-year marriage with the Hungarians has failed. We must part ways."
Andrej Hlinka, Catholic priest, leader of the Slovak People's Party, May 1918

Although by the late nineteenth century Slovaks had their own literary language and increasingly strong feelings of separate nationhood, Slovak politics stagnated under persistent Hungarian efforts at Magyarization in the dual Austro-Hungarian state formed in 1867. Thus, some Slovak politicians began to look for support abroad—particularly among the Czechs, who themselves were ruled by the Austrians. The presence of Slovak students in Prague and the situation of Slovaks in Upper Hungary resulted in a positive response from some of the Czech intelligentsia, but their overall view of Slovaks was sentimental and romantic, if not patronizing. Czechs tended to view the Slovak language as a mere dialect of Czech Slav. On the other hand, Slovaks looked to Prague with envy—it was the cultural, political, and national center that Slovakia lacked—and they also realized that the Czechs were the only neighbors with whom they might cooperate in the pursuit of national development.

Increased tensions between the Slovaks and the Hungarian authorities were illustrated most vividly in the massacre of Černová in October 1907. Fifteen Slovaks died in Černová when troops fired indiscriminately into a crowd that was trying to stop Magyar clergy from consecrating a new village church (the villagers wanted Slovak clergy to attend the consecration). Meanwhile, prominent Czech politicians began proposing the political union of Czechs and Slovaks in 1914. One year later, Tomáš G. Masaryk—who was half Slovak, but apparently knew little of this part of his heritage—made the union of Czechs and Slovaks an objective of Czech politics, claiming that, "the Slovaks are Bohemians in spite of their using their dialect as their literary language." Thus, elements of both the Slovak and the Czech political agendas began to take on a Czechoslovak orientation.

With the outbreak of the First World War in 1914, strong Slovak communities in the USA began making headway with the idea of a Czecho-Slovak union. Mass Czech and Slovak defections from the Austro-Hungarian armies helped to buttress the notion that such a union was possible. Still, Slovaks were generally unprepared when Great Britain and the USA officially recognized and supported the creation of a new Czecho-Slovak state in October 1918. The three main political actors in the founding of the Czechoslovak Republic were Masaryk, Edvard Beneš (Czech), and Milan Rastislav Štefánik (Slovak). For Slovaks, the most important of these was Štefánik, who was a remarkably skilled diplomat, and through whose connections Masaryk and Beneš were able to meet and obtain support from important personalities within the Triple Entente (Britain, France, and Russia). But in early

1919, just after the end of the First World War, Štefánik quarreled with Beneš and Masaryk over the position of Slovakia within Czechoslovakia. His sudden death in a plane crash only weeks later, along with the preceding quarrels, contributed to Slovak suspicions toward the Czechs during the First Republic of Czechoslovakia.

The severing of Slovakia from Hungary meant that Slovaks were catapulted from one political system into another with very little preparation, no public debate, and very few experienced political leaders. Underprepared, the Slovaks came to play second fiddle in the new state, enabling the Czechs, who had long received higher education in their own language, to carry out, largely, their own agenda. Where under the Hungarians the Slovaks had for a long time maintained their own national identity and individuality, under the new Czech agenda they discovered that they were not recognized as a nation, or even as a national minority, but as a mere branch of a new nation.

The First Slovak Republic and the National Uprising

By the end of the 1930s, the first Czechoslovak state was in a precarious position. Instability arose due to the Slovaks' discontent with their limited influence in political life, and to the rise of the opposing universalist ideologies of communism in Russia and fascism in Germany. With a significant German minority population, Czechoslovakia became a target of Hitler's determination to unite all Germans in Europe in one state. The Western powers were slow to counter Hitler's aggressive diplomacy, and Czechoslovakia fell into the German sphere of interest.

Feeling vulnerable, and not believing that the Czechoslovak state could, or would, defend the interests of Slovakia, Slovak nationalist politicians proposed the secession of Slovakia in October 1938. The Italian and German foreign ministers met in Vienna in November and redrew the frontiers of Slovak territory in Czechoslovakia, ceding significant territory to Hungary (including Nové Zámky, Šurany, and Košice), Poland (including Orava and Spiš), and German-occupied Austria (Devín, where the Morava and Danube rivers meet). With no recourse to Western support against the Germans, some Slovak politicians made the fateful decision to deal with the Nazis directly in February–March 1939, without Prague's approval. Prague responded by trying to secure Czecho-Slovak unity with a plan to have Czech troops occupy Slovak territory. This plan, although never carried out, surprised the Slovaks and prompted Third Reich officials to offer Slovakia an ultimatum—declare independence, or be left to an uncertain fate. The common state of the Czechs and Slovaks ceased to exist in 1939.

Although the new Slovak state was declared in a time of peace, its fate became directly tied to the Second World War, which broke out just five months later. In pursuit of the politics of survival, Slovak officials had two options—to organize the state according to the needs and traditions of the Slovak people, but risk German intervention; or to accept German fascism so that Germany would not have a reason to end Slovak independence. Thus, the Slovak experiment in statehood became dominated, and in the end marred, by ideological considerations. German priorities, as witnessed in Slovak participation in the Third Reich's campaign to eliminate the Jews in Central Europe, took precedence in official Slovak foreign policy—essentially characterizing Slovakia as a Nazi puppet state.

Beginning in early 1942, the Slovak government participated in the evacuation of some 70,000 Jews (two-thirds of the Jewish population in Slovakia at the time) to Nazi concentration camps, where most were killed. The deportations provoked opposition within Slovakia, from Catholics and Lutherans alike.

The Slovak National Uprising, an armed insurrection against the fascist Slovak government of the day, took place in 1944. In addition to Slovaks of various political and religious backgrounds, combatants included Soviet partisans, escaped French POWs, British Special Operations Executives, and American operatives from the Office of Strategic Services (a precursor to the CIA). Nonetheless, the resistance was put down by Nazi forces. As reprisal against the uprising, the Nazis destroyed

102 villages across Slovakia and executed more than 5,000 Slovaks, Jews, and Roma. Only one of these villages—Kalište—was never rebuilt. The remains of Kalište, where villagers were shot as they emerged from their houses and the buildings were burned to the ground five days before the Soviet Army liberated the area, is today an open-air museum and monument managed by the Museum of the Slovak National Uprising (located in nearby Banská Bystrica). Not well known outside Slovakia, the National Uprising played an important role in postwar Slovakia and Slovaks' sense of identity.

After the Second World War

Having been liberated from Nazi occupation by the Soviet Army, Slovakia once again became part of a reformed Czechoslovakia in May 1945. However, real independence was not in the cards. During postwar negotiations among the Allied Forces, it was agreed that Czechoslovakia would fall within the Soviet Union's sphere of influence. The 1946 Czechoslovak elections brought the Communist Party to power and by 1948 all political opposition was quashed. The communists put the country behind the Iron Curtain for forty years. Stalinist trials in the 1950s were staged to purge the Communist Party of members not considered hard-line enough. These trials terrorized the Czechoslovak people, and led many to retreat from public life. Slovak territories became subject to large-scale industrialization and collectivization, still visible today in the mass prefabricated concrete housing projects known as *paneláky*.

Pressure for social change resulted in the so-called Prague Spring of 1968. Led by Alexander Dubček, a Slovak, the state's control of the economy and political thought was loosened, giving hope to many Czechoslovaks that "socialism with a human face" was possible. Dubček's efforts resulted in a brief period where the arts and creativity flourished and links to the West were loosened. But the Prague Spring was quashed violently by the armies of the Warsaw Pact, with the invasion of Prague and Bratislava in August 1968. What followed was a period known as "normalization," with the Soviets taking a more active role in cracking down on dissidents.

The Velvet Revolution

Slovaks and Czechs languished under hard-line communism until late 1989, when the decay of the Soviet empire and the decline of communist ideas led to unrest and revolution around Central and Eastern Europe. In November 1989, a peaceful student demonstration was suppressed by riot police, who attacked the demonstrators with sticks. This led to further demonstrations under the guidance of Dubček and Václav Havel, characterized by protesters jingling their keys in town squares to symbolize the unlocking of doors, which in turn led to the end of communism in Czechoslovakia. This came to be known as the "Velvet Revolution," because the Communist Party was stripped of its powers without significant bloodshed and with no casualties (Havel's fondness for the rock group The Velvet Underground apparently inspired the name).

Czechoslovakia No More: the Velvet Divorce

"... in discussing the past or present, one more properly speaks of a Czech heritage and a Slovak heritage that are occasionally identical, frequently similar, but more often than not different in important respects."

Bruce M. Garver, "The Czechoslovak Tradition," in Czechoslovakia: The Heritage of Ages Past, 1979

Growing feelings of national identity and political tensions between Slovak and Czech politicians—chiefly former Slovak Prime Minister Vladimir Mečiar and former Czech Prime Minister Václav Klaus—(characterized by the so-called "Hyphen War" debate about what the country should be called: Czechoslovakia, the Czech preference; or Czecho-Slovakia, the Slovak preference) led to a parliamentary decision to split Czechoslovakia into the Czech Republic and Slovakia on January 1, 1993—an event sometimes referred to as the "Velvet Divorce." A public referendum was never held, and at the time opinion polls indicated that only about 9 percent of Czechoslovaks supported the break. Nonetheless, the breakup of Czechoslovakia encountered little resistance (and occurred with little fanfare) and, in the years since the Velvet Divorce, generally most people in both countries have indicated their support for the separate republics.

The newly reborn Slovak Republic initially struggled under Mečiar's authoritarian-style leadership (often referred to as "Mečiarism"), but a series of reform-minded coalition governments after 1998 (led by Mikuláš Dzurinda until 2006) resulted in Slovakia's becoming a member of NATO and the European Union in 2004. Despite these steps forward as an independent country, many foreigners still hold fast to the notion of Czechoslovakia. Perhaps because the map of Central Europe has often changed throughout the twentieth century, or perhaps due to the lack of fanfare around Czechoslovakia's peaceful breakup, or because the Czechs always tended to dominate over the

Slovaks and inherited the most experience of international statehood after the Velvet Divorce, even otherwise well-educated foreigners still make the mistake of referring to Czechoslovakia as though it still existed. The fact that the Czechs kept the old Czechoslovak flag is also a source of confusion. During Czechoslovak times, the blue triangular shape on the flag represented Slovakia, but the Czechs nowadays claim it represents Moravia. The flag was a major source of conflict between the two Republics in 1992, and continues to be a source of potential confusion internationally. Such confusion leads many in the know to observe that Slovakia remains a largely unknown and underappreciated country.

A CZECH VIEW OF THE SLOVAKS

"In the Central European context, the Czechs always tended to regard everybody else as underdeveloped peasants of whom only the Slovaks were civilizable—and only if they wanted to live with Czechs, behave like Czechs, and be grateful to Czechs for having once rescued them from national annihilation at the hands of the Hungarians. Now that the ever so ungrateful Slovaks have decided to go it alone, the Czechs have written them off, too, and consigned them into that vague, uninteresting, indistinguishable mass of East European peasantry . . . . The Slovaks themselves approach everyone with suspicion, assuming everyone is there to rip them off, because they know that everyone has already ripped them off, and everyone owes them something. And by everyone, they mean everyone."

Benjamin Kuras, Czech-English writer, *Is There Life on Marx?* 2001

REAL CHANGE: 1998, NOT 1989

"For Slovakia . . . the biggest historical event is not 1989 but 1998. November '89 didn't originate in Bratislava; it came from Prague. Yes, it was on the same day, but we know very well that Prague was the engine of those changes. We knew that in Slovakia we wouldn't be able to do it without Prague. But 1998 was the only historical event when the Slovaks had to fulfill their own task, their own duty. That's why I think that Slovakia changed on that very date. It brought some self-confidence, which for this nation was very crucial. Slovaks don't remember 1998 as the crucial moment that it was. They will see it in the future, in the long run."

Martin M. Šimečka, author and journalist, referring to the country ridding itself of Mečiarism politics, August 2009

GOVERNMENT

Slovakia is a democratic republic, with a multiparty system. Legislative powers are vested in the elected parliament, the

150-seat National Council of the Slovak Republic, with delegates elected for four-year terms on the basis of proportional representation; executive powers are exercised by the government led by the prime minister; the judiciary is independent of the executive and the legislature; and the head of state is the president. The president is elected directly by popular vote under the two-round system for a five-year term, and is eligible for a second term. Following National Council elections the leader of the majority party, or of a majority coalition, is normally appointed prime minister by the president. The governing Cabinet is appointed by the president on the recommendation of the prime minister, but has to receive a majority in parliament.

Slovak citizens are eligible to vote at the age of eighteen, and the country has universal, equal, and direct suffrage by secret ballot. Similar to the Netherlands, Slovakia is a single, multimember constituency. Voters indicate their preferred candidates on a semi-open list, and parties must pass the 5 percent election threshold to be eligible to form part of the parliament.

POLITICS

Many Slovaks are generally skeptical of politics and politicians. Perhaps as a consequence of high expectations after 1989, and often disappointing or too slow results, or due to the cynical and sometimes criminal behavior of some of the country's politicians, they don't believe that real political change is possible. Election turnouts, therefore, have been steadily declining since the early 1990s (with the exception of the 2010 election, which saw a slight increase in voter turnout) and sociopolitical activism is almost nonexistent. There are still, astonishingly, a lot of people in Slovakia who are not ready to sign, for example, a political petition. Although they may agree with its content, they may be reluctant to sign it because they are afraid that somebody might use the information against them. And one is still likely to hear, even from otherwise aware and educated people, that they "don't want anything to do with politics." On the Slovak political scene the standard terms of political science—conservatism, liberalism, and social democracy—generally don't apply. A typical characterization of Slovak political parties is that "they are indefinable bastards," more or less, of course. The mixing and matching of political ideologies that characterizes Slovak politics is in large part due to the number of political parties (more than twenty) that exist and the necessity for coalition-building in forming a government. There is a wide spectrum of political parties—new parties arise and old parties cease to exist or merge at a frequent rate. The outgoing prime minister Robert Fico (2006–10) used the word *zlepenec* (which literally means a glued-together bunch of hair or a geological conglomerate) to describe the mix of "right-wing" liberal-conservative parties (as they are labeled by the Slovak media, at least) that formed a coalition after the 2010 elections, thus ousting him from power. However, the incoming coalition was no more a *zlepenec* than the previous ruling coalition of Fico's socialist/populist party with ultranationalist and nationalist conservative partners, including the infamous Vladimír Mečiar.

In many Western European and North American political cultures, the political left tends to stand for change, but in postcommunist states like Slovakia, the reverse is true—the political right signifies change. The victory of the liberal-conservative coalition in the 2010 elections, therefore, was in many ways a victory for young voters over the elderly, inspiring many young Slovaks to observe that, "this election was different." Perhaps for the first time since the Velvet Divorce, young Slovaks felt optimistic and in control of their future, which they had previously felt was mostly controlled by an elderly, backward-looking electorate. The 2010 elections were significant in that Slovakia gained its first female prime minister, Dr. Iveta Radičová; the ultranationalist Slovak National Party saw a significant drop in its election results (despite tensions with Hungarians leading up to the election); and Vladimír Mečiar, the country's most notorious politician, was finally ousted from parliament. The cabinet that emerged from these elections is also the first since 1989 not to include former Communist Party members.

Political Skepticism

The skepticism that many Slovaks feel toward politics and politicians is illustrated by the fact that in almost every election there are allegations that one or more political parties pay members of the Roma community, which normally has very low voter turnout rates, for their votes. Such allegations are almost always in relation to Roma in East Slovakia, where unemployment and economic difficulty persist. Such stories do little, unfortunately, to improve the image of the Slovak Roma, eastern Slovakia, or politicians in general.

THE ECONOMY

As recently as early 2008, Slovakia's economy was described as the "Tatra tiger" or the "Detroit of the East." Before the global economic downturn of 2008, these were appropriate labels for a country with one of the highest economic growth rates in the EU and one of the highest per capita automobile production rates in the world. But the nature of Slovakia's economy—small, open, and pro-export oriented—meant that its good fortunes were massively influenced by the conditions of its largest trading partners in the West, particularly the USA. By the end of 2008—due in part to the collapse of financial giants in the USA, and in part due to government spending at the time—Slovakia's economy had slowed and unemployment rates rose dramatically. A car-scrapping bonus, similar to those employed in the USA and Germany, was implemented in late 2008 to keep the second-largest Slovak industry—car manufacturing—afloat. Nonetheless, it is clear that the Slovak economy has a long road to recovery ahead.

Despite the global economic downturn, Slovakia became the first country among the Visegrad Group (which also includes Hungary, the Czech Republic, and Poland) to adopt the euro as its currency. Economic observers described the switch from the Slovak koruna to the euro as "exemplarily smooth." It is notable that this transition occurred less than twenty years after the collapse of the communist-era Council for Mutual Economic Assistance (COMECON), under which Slovakia's economy had been centrally planned and completely isolated from the outside modern market economy. Because much of the country's industrialization took place during the communist era, many Slovak industries produced goods that were not competitive in the world market. Also, in communist days the Slovak economy was dominated by the production of weapons and military equipment. This industry had employed as much as 10 percent of the Slovak workforce in the 1980s, and the Czechoslovak government's decision in the early 1990s to drastically reduce the country's defense industry compounded the problem of outmoded industry in Slovakia, contributing to high unemployment rates.

Following the Velvet Divorce in 1993, Slovakia's economy made the transition from a centrally planned economy to a free market economy, resulting in massive privatization whereby state properties were transferred into private hands, often in dubious circumstances. The period between 1994 and 1998—under the leadership of Vladimir Mečiar—has been called an era of "crony capitalism," characterized by friends and family members of corrupt government officials benefiting from privatization schemes. Reform-minded governments since 1998 have more or less sharply cut public spending and introduced massive reforms, including a 20 percent flat rate for VAT (value-added tax), income, and corporate taxes.

With a strong, skills-based workforce, Slovakia's industry today is dominated by the automotive, mechanical engineering, metallurgy, chemical engineering, electronics, and information technology sectors. Until 2008, the automotive industry was the fastest-growing sector. Foreign investors in the Slovak market include PSA Peugeot Citroen, Volkswagen, US Steel, Sony, Samsung, and Enel. The banking industry is also dominated by foreign ownership.

Regardless of Slovakia's recent "Tatra tiger" status, unemployment rates in the country have remained consistently among the highest in Europe for the past two decades—from a low of 7.7 percent in 2008 and a high of 20 percent in 1998. Unemployment remains the Achilles heel of the Slovak economy. The majority of the unemployed have lower levels of education than the national average. Unemployment is particularly high in eastern Slovakia, where economic growth has lagged behind the rest of the country.

With an estimated (2009) labor force of 2.641 million, 69.4 percent of the employed work in services, 27 percent in industry, and 3.5 percent in agriculture. Main export commodities include machinery and electrical equipment (35.9 percent), vehicles (21 percent), base metals (11.3 percent), chemicals and minerals (8.1 percent), and plastics (4.9 percent) (2009 estimates). Slovakia's main trading partners are Germany and the Czech Republic.

SLOVAKS ABROAD

Slovaks have long played a part in the shaping of Central Europe, and the first Slovaks who traveled overseas to the USA and Canada, for example, did so in the nineteenth century, when these North American nations were at a critical point in their formation. However, due to historical problems of statistical definition (Slovaks have been variously labeled "Czechoslovak," "Austro-Hungarian," and "Slav"), the number of Slovaks living outside Slovakia has been estimated by the newspaper *SME* at between 1.5 and 2.3 million. Significant Slovak expatriate communities exist in the Czech Republic, the USA, Canada, and the Vojvodina region of Serbia, and some thousands of Slovaks currently live and work in the United Kingdom and Ireland. The Slovak Statistics Office put the number of native-born Slovak nationals working abroad at 124,600 in the second quarter of 2009.

In May 2010, in reaction to the amended Citizenship Act passed in Hungary—which would allow around two million ethnic Hungarians in Central and Eastern Europe to gain Hungarian citizenship more easily, if they so chose—the Slovak cabinet amended the Slovak Citizenship Act. The proposed Slovak amendment, anticipated to become law in early 2011, says that a Slovak citizen who voluntarily obtains citizenship in another country will lose Slovak citizenship, ruling out the possibility of dual citizenship for those who have emigrated abroad. The government that came to power in July 2010 has indicated that these retaliatory measures against the Hungarians may be withdrawn.

PROMINENT SLOVAKS ABROAD

The following well-known individuals all have some Slovak heritage.

Štefan Banič (1870–1941), inventor of the parachute (born in Smolenice)
John Dopyera (1893–1988), inventor of the dobro guitar (born in Dolná Krupá)
Ladislav Hudec (1893–1958), prominent architect in Shanghai, China (born in Banská Bystrica)
Paul Newman (1925–2008), actor (Slovak mother)
Andy Warhol (1928–1987), artist/filmmaker (Slovak parents)
Stan Mikita (1940–), retired NHL hockey player (born in Sokolče)
Tom Selleck (1945–), actor (Slovak father)
Edita Grúberová (1946–), opera singer (born in Bratislava)
Peter Šťastný (1956–), retired NHL hockey player, EU politician (born in Bratislava)
Peter Breiner (1957–), composer, conductor, and pianist (born in Humenné)
Marián Hossa (1979–), NHL hockey player (born in Stará Ľubovňa)
Martina Hingis (1980–), retired professional tennis player (born in Košice)

chapter **two**

VALUES & ATTITUDES

While all generalizations should be taken with a grain of salt, it is possible to characterize the Slovak people as quietly proud, practical, and enduring. Although many Slovaks describe themselves as resistant to change, their nation has undergone significant, often turbulent changes in the last hundred years. Slovaks have adapted to these rifts with a unique combination of careful flexibility, patience, and modesty. Modern-day Slovaks look to their nation's future with a critical eye, wary of being over optimistic, but they are not weighed down by self-criticism. Rarely boisterous or very emotional, they have a growing sense of connection with, and of their place within, the European community. And, despite their apparent reluctance to change, Slovak society has continued in recent years to be characterized by flux—economically, socially, and politically.

FAMILY

The family is probably the most important factor in the lives of the vast majority of Slovaks. Most households, in fact, have two family members—normally either a young couple who has not yet had children or an elderly couple whose children have moved away. Households with four members—usually two parents and two children—are the next most common. Young adults studying away from home will generally return home on weekends, and in some cases the location of their studies is even determined by their relative distance from their family. For financial and social reasons, young couples tend to live near their parents and, unless moving away is necessary for work or study purposes, immediate family members tend to live in the same town or city, or at least in the same region.

The family in contemporary Slovak life is important in large part because of the country's recent political past. Before 1989, finding fulfillment in public life was all but impossible unless one were a member of the Communist Party. Travel was restricted, political activism was severely discouraged, and private enterprise was illegal. Therefore, the family was one of the few areas in which one could achieve personal goals, and Slovaks tended to find refuge at home from what was generally a hypocritical and oppressive public life. In the 1970s, for example, getting married and having children as soon as possible was the norm for young people. The communist government of the day offered lengthy maternity leave and attractive tax incentives for married couples, including allowances for childbirth. And since it was nearly impossible for single persons or childless couples to secure a flat, communism actually strengthened family ties and intergenerational bonds.

WORK ETHIC

Although nothing outweighs the importance of the family for Slovaks, work certainly rates a very close second. After the shift from a centrally planned economy to a market economy, Slovakia, like many former communist states, experienced significant changes in the world of work. Full employment was replaced by a rapid rise in unemployment and intensive labor emigration. More than other Europeans, Slovaks consider work to be a "very important" part of their lives. When asked, most Slovaks will characterize work as "absolutely necessary," meaning that their personal finances and access to capital (through family ties, for example) are not extensive and work is essential to survival. As such, Slovaks tend to take a very practical approach to employment, rather than an idealistic one. Many young people tend to choose a particular career because it is highly paid, with good job security, rather than because they have a particular vocation for it, or interest in it.

In the socialist era there was no unemployment—in fact it was illegal. Slovak society has thus struggled to some degree in dealing with the psychological and social problems often associated with unemployment in a capitalist economy—depression, mental illness, and alcoholism. Having a secure job before 1989 was not something that many Slovaks worried about, but in the last twenty years finding well-paid work has taken on a very high value for the vast majority of the population. Anxiety over losing one's job also means that many Slovaks put up with uncongenial conditions. Complaining about the boss, or colleagues, or too much work for too little money, is common. Where a foreigner would sooner quit a job than continue in a bad working environment, many Slovaks endure the hardships rather than face unemployment. Studies have found, for example, that Slovaks rank above the European average in following orders from their bosses even when they do not agree with them—further supporting the notion that keeping one's job is more important than enjoying or taking pride in one's work.

Anxiety about finding or keeping a job also means that many Slovaks hold negative attitudes toward immigrant workers. A 2001 research survey found that 88 percent of respondants agreed with the statement, "when jobs are scarce, employers should give priority to nationals over immigrants," whereas in Sweden only 11 percent agreed.

Reflecting these attitudes, many recent university graduates, for example, will commonly work long hours in an effort to make ends meet or impress their bosses, or both. It is not unusual for a young professional to leave home at 6:00 a.m. and return late in the evening.

Those who do decide to leave a difficult working environment, or who find themselves unemployed, may become self-employed entrepreneurs. Private firms and small businesses are quite common.

Although work is considered a very important part of Slovak life, Slovaks know how to balance their work and leisure time quite well. Annual holidays in the Tatra Mountains or Croatia, for example, are savored, as are weekends.

THE AFTERMATH OF COMMUNISM

"The collapse of communism has not led to an end of history."
Yale Richardson, *From Da to Yes*, 1995

More than twenty years have passed since the fall of communism and the Velvet Revolution in what was then Czechoslovakia, but forty years of enforced socialism have left an indelible mark on Slovakia, signs of which are still very much present. The outward architectural evidence of communism is easy to spot, particularly in the innumerable ugly apartment complexes, or *paneláky* (the most dramatic example of which may be in the Bratislava suburb of Petržalka) and *domy kultúry* (Culture Houses) prevalent in the old city squares of most towns and cities. More subtle signifiers of communism, noticeable in both individual and collective behavior, will also be apparent to the observant visitor.

FATALISM AND PASSIVITY

Subtle personal traits that betray the political and social history of Slovakia throughout much of the twentieth century include a moderate degree of fatalism and passivity toward change. Such attitudes were perhaps most vividly apparent in the Slovak reactions to the breakup of Czechoslovakia in 1993. As we have seen, only about 9 percent of Czechs and Slovaks supported the Velvet Divorce at the time, and political leaders in both countries divided Czechoslovakia without holding a public referendum or asking for the people's support. Regardless of the low levels of support for it outside political circles, the breakup of Czechoslovakia met no resistance. Although some Slovaks will still murmur today that the breakup was a "bad idea for Slovakia," this sentiment is generally accompanied by a shrug of the shoulders, as if to say "but what can I do about it?"

Such passive acceptance can be attributed in part to the forty years of communism that Slovaks endured. During this period, few had the courage to speak up, let alone act upon their opinions. Nowadays Slovaks are more likely to voice their views—usually in the form of complaining—but still relatively few take political or social action. A public opinion poll in late 2009, for example, found that 55 percent of Slovaks agreed with the sentiment that success in life is determined by forces outside one's control.

Communist-Era Humor

Old communist-era humor still has an audience in Slovakia. For example, "How do you get a mole out of your garden? You should put an application for the Communist Party down its hole, and there will be only two possibilities—the mole will sign the form and immediately stop working; or, he will refuse to sign it, emigrate, and start working in your neighbor's garden."

SELF-CRITICISM

Related to this passivity is the apparently rather critical attitude that some Slovaks hold toward their country and people. However, this should not be read as dismissive of Slovakia in general. Rather, it is a manifestation of the complaining culture that rarely translates into action. When met with challenges, or when finding some aspect of their society wanting, Slovaks seldom hesitate to say something about it, but action is not so forthcoming. To the uninitiated foreigner this seeming negativity and apathy can appear to do something of a disservice to Slovakia, or be poor self-promotion, when in fact such criticism is inspired by a desire or aspiration to see the country continue to develop in positive ways.

DISILLUSIONMENT AND NOSTALGIA

Public opinion surveys conducted twenty years after the fall of communism in late 2009 indicated that about 70 percent of Slovaks approved of the change to a democratic system of governance and about 65 percent approved of the change to a capitalist economy. On the other hand, the prevailing view was that people were generally better off economically under communism. Furthermore, there was a general consensus that ordinary people benefit far less under democracy and capitalism than business owners and politicians, and only about 43 percent of Slovaks in 2009 indicated that they embraced democratic values (a fair judiciary, multiparty elections, free media, free religion, free speech, and so on). When surveyed in 1991 about whether or not the state was run for the benefit of all people, 71 percent of Slovaks agreed; but in 2009, when asked the same question, only 33 percent agreed. These figures point to a growing disillusionment and dissatisfaction with democracy and capitalism only twenty years after the fall of communism, and support the trend, particularly among the older generation, of sentimentalizing communist times.

Such sentimentalism is evident in the continued popularity of some old communist-era products that continue to thrive commercially, such as Kofola (a cola), Horalky (a peanut and chocolate wafer bar), Vinea (a carbonated grape-based soft drink), and Sójové rezy (a soy-based treat). Such products, although their producers are steadfastly capitalist, have been described by some as reflecting a kind of nostalgia for communist times. Others will simply tell you that they remain popular because they taste good, or are better than multinational Western brands.

CONSPIRACY THEORY?

Although the feeling is no longer as widespread as it was in the decade immediately after the Velvet Revolution, some Slovaks will tell you with absolute conviction that the events of November 1989 were orchestrated by members of the Communist Party and the ŠtB (Štátna bezpečnosť, a plainclothes secret state security police force similar to the KGB). According to this theory, a bungled plot by communist reformers took place—in other words, communist reformers ordered the police attack so as to provoke mass protest, which in turn would force the party's hard-liners to resign and give way to reformist leadership.

As evidence, those who subscribe to this possibility will point to former members of the Communist Party, many of whom are among the richest people in Slovakia today, and many of whom are still involved in politics, and to the fact that no communists were punished for their crimes. Several unanswered questions remain regarding to what extent the events of 1989 were spontaneous or the result of a plot.

A GROWING CONSUMER CULTURE

The younger generation—particularly those below the age of thirty, who have little or no memory of communist times—tend to look upon democracy and capitalism as mere synonyms for "freedom." Many young Slovaks demonstrate little or no social or political commitment, and seem to live in a world apart from their parents and grandparents. The concerns of this postcommunist generation of youth amount to little more than friends and fun, where "freedom" is equivalent to the freedom to buy, free of conscience and responsibility. Mass, often uncritical, consumerism is the social norm of the day—behavior that sets this generation apart dramatically, for better or worse, and suggests that the future of Slovakia will continue to be marked by change.

DISAFFECTED YOUTH

The decline in social awareness demonstrated by the postcommunist generation of youth is perhaps most vividly displayed in the plague of graffiti that is evident in both urban and rural settings throughout Slovakia, and was almost nonexistent prior to 1989. Little seems to be being done by police, parents, or other authority figures that effectively dissuades the young from vandalizing public and private property in this way. Likewise, little effort is made to cover or clean it up, leaving otherwise pleasant buildings (and just as often less pleasant buildings) hideously scarred.

TO SA NEDÁ

Due in large part to their history of always being under the rule of someone else—whether Hungarians, Czechs, communists, or now Brussels—Slovaks have tended to perceive themselves as victims. This is especially true among the over-forties, who remember well what life was like before 1989. Complaining is thus something of a national sport, particularly for older people, and whether it's true or not, many Slovaks feel put upon by others and envious of those who have more, or who seem to be more successful. Bureaucracy under communism—traces of which can still be detected to this day—was often arbitrary, and led to a kind of lazy arrogance or indifference toward the public, encapsulated in the response to seemingly simple requests, "*To sa nedá,*" or "*To nejde*," "It can't be done."

This kind of passive aggression on the part of bureaucrats has been explained as resulting from the fact that Slovaks historically were rarely able to exercise political choice, and their fate was often determined by external influences. Thus until very recently Slovaks seldom, if ever, experienced politics as a consequence of their own choices, leading to a generally weak sense of political responsibility, to a "lack of repentance," as the politician Emil Komárik has characterized it.

On the other side of *to sa nedá*, Slovaks know very well how to work the system—another legacy of their rule by external forces. They excel at using their charm, hospitality, and personal contacts. As a way of breaking the ice, or getting things started, it is not uncommon to offer a gift or small token of appreciation (such as a bottle of alcohol, or flowers). These gifts are normally meant to symbolize or bring about a sense of partnership or bonding, rather than being outright bribes.

SERVICE WITHOUT A SMILE

North American and Western European visitors to Slovakia will quickly notice that the saying, "the customer is always right" does not universally apply in Slovakia. Although the situation is changing, with increased foreign business influence and employees and bosses with international experience, a good many shop assistants, waiting staff, "bureaucrats behind windows," and other such people dealing with the public will rarely give service with a smile. Similarly, don't be surprised, in response to what might seem like a simple request, to hear "*To sa nedá*" or "*Neviem*" ("I don't know"). Individuals in customer service positions will rarely go out of their way for a customer, or potential customer, and when asked for help are likely to do so grudgingly, or with bad grace.

Such attitudes are largely a legacy of the country's socialist and communist past. In days gone by, when service personnel were paid more or less the same low wages whether or not a customer even entered their shop, there was little incentive to approach a potential customer with enthusiasm or even basic politeness. And although Slovakia has changed to a capitalist economy since 1989, and consumerism is on the rise, some behavior has been slow to catch up. This is not simply generational—young people learn this behavior from their parents, teachers, and bosses. The notion that friendly customer service can go a long way to increasing sales is still foreign to many Slovaks (as in many other postcommunist states). The apparent increase in consumerism as a hobby in and of itself, however, suggests that Slovak shoppers are unfazed by poor customer service, and until shoppers themselves demand better the situation is unlikely to change much. Areas accustomed to foreign visitors show signs of moving toward a more recognizably capitalist service approach, but this is not yet widespread outside Bratislava and the popular tourist sites. On the other hand, visitors who are sick of persistent and aggressive salespeople badgering them to buy something they don't need or want may find the more apathetic Slovak variety refreshingly welcome.

Real estate agents, for example, rather than actively trying to sell a property, generally wait for customers to come to them, and even after initial contact is made don't necessarily take an active role in trying to seal the deal. Similarly, restaurant staff often appear to be in no hurry to serve, and the friendly "Are you enjoying your meal?" that North Americans are used to hearing is pretty much unheard in Slovakia.

WEALTH AND MONEY

As the Slovak economy has moved over to market-driven capitalism over the last twenty years, the gap between rich and poor has broadened considerably. Under communism, everyone was essentially equal when it came to work and finances. But with the fall of communism, the upper and lower limits on earnings have disappeared. Consumerism and materialism have become something of a sport for those with money (or those who like to appear to have it), and the accumulation of wealth is often accompanied by the ostentatious display of expensive cars, clothing, or houses. Nonexistent just a few years ago, shopping malls are now considered the place to be for a growing number of Slovak consumers.

Hard work and wealth, however, do not necessarily follow hand-in-hand, and professions that garner considerable respect and reasonable salaries in other countries are in Slovakia often very poorly paid. Medical doctors and teachers at all levels, however hardworking, are the most notorious examples. This results in a situation where fewer young Slovaks aspire to practice medicine or teach than is the case in other countries. The Slovak *nouveaux riches* are most often entrepreneurs, politicians, or local mafia. Sometimes these designations are not mutually exclusive.

Mortgages, bank loans, and the credit culture in general are very new in Slovakia. Until very recently Slovaks had no notion of borrowing money from a bank to buy a house, apartment, or car. Loans to attend university are still largely unheard of (universities are heavily state-subsidized, resulting in free or very low tuition costs). In days gone by, if Slovaks borrowed money at all it was from their parents, and in return probably cared for them when they were elderly. (State pensions, to this day, are very meager.) A healthy wariness of debt is still common among average citizens, and there are many who live frugally, but more and more are now grasping the idea of borrowing money on credit, and this is reflected in the fast-growing number of expensive cars, clothing, and lavishly built or renovated homes.

Until recently, few Slovaks understood that the common depiction of Westerners as living in big houses and driving fancy cars is a reflection of a borrowing and credit culture. What a Slovak may call a "credit card" is still, in fact, what a North American calls a "debit card"—the funds must be in the account for the card to be used. Thus, the perception of the rich foreigner persists, and Westerners may be overcharged or shortchanged because they are assumed to be able to afford it.

MEN AND WOMEN

Men and women in Slovakia generally keep to traditional gender roles and stereotypes. Women tend to be ultrafeminine, particularly in their dress, in some cases almost to the point of coming across as flaunting their sexuality; men, in recent years, have become more fashion conscious, and this is particularly true among those in their teens and twenties. Materialism, particularly when it comes to fashion accessories like shoes, is on the rise among the young, both male and female. In June 2010, Slovaks elected their first female Prime Minister, Dr. Iveta Radičová—who had also, by the way, become Slovakia's first female professor of sociology in 2005—but the participation of women in post-1989 political life has consistently been very low, and women are more likely to be unemployed than men.

Notions of female beauty, even among women themselves, are more stereotypically entrenched in Slovakia than many Westerners are accustomed to. More women are slim than not, and they are almost always well dressed and groomed, leading many foreigners—particularly men—to agree with the generally accepted belief that, "Slavic women are the most beautiful in the world." Hair coloring, tanning, and makeup are very common among women of all ages. The vast majority of Slovak women above the age of fifteen will color their hair on a regular basis, to the point that, when asked, a woman will tell you with a smile that she no longer knows what her natural color is. Many old ladies favor blue, pink, or purple hair. Similarly, few Slovak women would ever leave the house without makeup or putting effort into their dress.

The representation of women in advertising tends to reflect or support these standards of female beauty. Scantily clad, stereotypically beautiful women are commonly featured in advertisements for products that in some cases have little or nothing to do with women as consumers. In other words, women tend to be depicted as more beauty than substance, and few Slovaks will raise an

eyebrow at this. The hypersexualized representation of young women in Slovak society is considered normal by most.

Slovak men have often been described—by foreign women, at least—as somewhat ordinary in appearance. Such labeling is perhaps unfair, and is probably only made in comparison to the above-average looks of Slovak women. The men do, however, tend to be more forward with women regarding sexual matters. Extramarital affairs between male bosses and female employees, for example,

are normally openly accepted, and affairs and infidelity are not always met with scorn or separation. Both men and women, it seems, tend to look the other way, or simply tolerate such extracurricular activities as merely youthful behavior, rather than cause for great concern. Attitudes toward nudity also tend to be relaxed. Nearly invisible bathing suits are often seen, on both sexes, at outdoor pools and lakes, and a degree of nudity is tolerated at many public beaches, although these are not labeled or advertised as nudist areas.

Apparently liberal attitudes to sexuality are not entirely universal. On the flip side, some Slovaks still exhibit old-fashioned, if not conservative, behavior in their dealings with the opposite sex. This is truer among older people. For example, when a man accompanies a woman on a walk, he should position himself on the outside, to shield her from passing traffic; a man opens doors for a woman and lets her pass through first, except when entering a restaurant, when he, as host, leads the way; and it is considered rude for a man to sit with his knees spread wide, or with one ankle resting on the other knee. However, such traditional good manners are becoming rare, particularly in big cities like Bratislava, where the gentlemanly behavior of old has all but disappeared.

As far as equality between the sexes is concerned, in the realm of economy and political life women in Slovakia are financially disadvantaged and outnumbered. For the last decade, for example, the difference in earnings between men and women has remained significant. Men, on average, earn between 25 and 30 percent more than women. This is due in large part to the nature of the paid work that women undertake.

Overwhelmingly, Slovak women work in the so-called traditional female spheres—health care, education, and the service industry—while men tend to be employed in the industrial, technical, and engineering fields, where higher wages are attainable. Women are further disadvantaged economically by their role as primary caregivers for children and other dependent family members. While Slovak men are now beginning to take greater part in child care, the responsibility for this is still overwhelmingly on women. On the positive side, women in Slovakia have a high degree of educational attainment, on a par with their male counterparts (although there are gender differences in fields of study), and boast a high standard of health and survival.

HIERARCHIES AND TITLES

Although formality among the younger generation is beginning to wane, most Slovaks are very polite, and address strangers in a formal manner. Furthermore, they generally take earned academic titles very seriously. This is particularly true in business and education situations. A university student, for example, will normally address an academic doctor as "*pán doktor*" (for a man) or "*pani doktorka*" (for a woman).

Doctoral graduates tend to use their academic titles even in informal environments, such as on Facebook, although the accepted use of such titles is generally limited to business and official communications. In day-to-day communication, people are normally addressed by their title only if they have introduced themselves using it (verbally, or by a business card), or if one wishes to express high respect. In addressing someone who is known to have a doctorate, it is best to use the formal title, or risk correction or possible complaint later. Where in many other countries such behavior might be considered snobbish or high-handed, in Slovakia such formalities are merely a sign of respect.

It is common knowledge, at least among the well educated, that if you identify yourself as holding an academic title, you will be treated with greater respect, for example, when visiting a hospital or medical doctor. Slovak doctors, in particular, attach value to titles. This could be related to the fact that both medical and academic professionals earn relatively low salaries for their levels of education—so it may reflect a kind of solidarity on the part of highly qualified, underpaid academics. (For common academic titles, see p. 147).

In addressing a person who does not have an official academic title, or where this is not known, the honorific titles *pán* (Mr.), *pani* (Mrs.), or *slečna* (Ms.) and the person's surname are used. Acquaintances may refer to each other using these honorific titles accompanied by first names, but foreign visitors are advised to wait to be invited before using someone's first name. Similarly, when greeting a stranger or mere acquaintance, a formal greeting such as "*Dobrý deň*" ("Good day") is preferred over the informal "*Ahoj*" ("Hello"). There is a rather strict protocol dictating when a particular greeting can be used (see page 89).

ATTITUDES TOWARD THE POLICE

Formality is the norm when addressing authority figures such as bureaucrats and police (*polícia*). Respect in these cases, however, may be only skin deep, as many Slovaks express considerable distrust and negative perceptions of bureaucracy and law enforcement agencies. The police in particular are widely considered to be lawbreakers themselves, and many Slovaks privately accuse police officers of having links to neo-Nazis, mafia, and other groups engaged in questionable practices. Although it is less and less common today, police regularly used to ask speeding drivers to pay cash on the spot, or risk being charged with a more serious offense. The authorities have done much to eliminate such practices in recent years, but widely held distrust of the police persists. This is a holdover from communist times, when the police were justifiably feared and avoided at all costs.

RELIGION

Freedom of religion is guaranteed in the Slovak constitution, and Slovaks are overwhelmingly Christian. Depending on which source one believes, most Slovaks (between 57.9 and 60.4 percent) identify themselves as Roman Catholics; 9.6 to 15.9 percent are nonreligious or atheist (significantly lower than in neighboring Czech Republic, where 65 percent identify as such); approximately 6 percent are Protestant; 3.4 to 5 percent are Greek Catholic; and 1.7 percent are Reform Christian. But despite these numbers, generally only one-third of Church members regularly attend services. Jews make up 0.04 percent of the contemporary Slovak population, but prior to the Second World War there were an estimated 90,000 (1.6 percent of the population). Major Christian denominations in Slovakia, in addition to those mentioned above, include the Evangelical Church of the Augsburg Confession, Jehovah's Witness, and Evangelical

Methodist. Smaller numbers of adherents follow other Christian denominations, including Baptists, the Brethren Church, Seventh-day Adventists, the Apostolic Church, the Christian Corps, and the Hussite Church.

REGIONAL AND NATIONAL PRIDE

Visitors may be surprised to learn that in this small country there are at least three strong—although unofficial—regional identities: East, Middle, and West Slovakia. Each region has its own linguistic dialect(s), and people are quite proud of their own region, commonly referring to it as part of their personal identity. Although Slovakia has been stereotyped by outsiders, such as in Hollywood films like *Eurotrip* and *Hostel*, each region in Slovakia is subject to its own stereotyping by those from other regions.

West Slovakia (and Záhorie)

The Slovaks have a love/hate relationship with Bratislava. Such feelings are articulated in the well-known song "Brďokoky" by the punk rock band Horkýže Slíže (Surely Not a Noodle), which makes fun of people from Bratislava and their manner of speaking and behavior. The widely popular hip-hop group Kontrafakt also use Bratislava as controversial fodder in their songs. Those from Trnava also have their own unique accents. More generally, the rest of Slovakia tends to look upon West Slovakia with a somewhat critical eye, typecasting the natives as believing that Slovakia's borders end with those of Bratislava.

People from Záhorie (sometimes referred to as Záhoráci) are a frequent target of region-specific jokes by the rest of Slovaks. This small subregion, lying to the west of the Carpathians, is known for its own linguistic dialect, similar to Moravian. Záhoráci are generally regarded as slow or obtuse, perhaps because many refuse to speak standard Slovak, even in situations where it would be appropriate. Also regarded as frugal, individualistic, and overly respectful of property, they are sometimes thus labeled as variously mean, egotistical, and greedy. In the past, the Záhorie region enjoyed lively trade relations with Austria (perhaps inspiring a degree of jealousy among other Slovaks), and young people from the region often served Austrian families.

Middle Slovakia

People from Middle Slovakia, and especially from the subregion of Orava, are generally thought by other Slovaks to be overly proud of their "Slovakness." Prominent contemporary members of the Slovak National Party, for example, have come from Middle Slovakia, and a sense of distrust—if not hostility—directed toward Bratislava is palpable here.

The middle Slovak linguistic dialect was codified by Ľudovít Štúr in 1843 and stands as the officially accepted form of the Slovak language. However, some linguistic differences still exist—*ba*, for example, indicates a strong "yes" in this region, while *áno* is the norm elsewhere.

East Slovakia

Slovaks from the east are normally easily distinguishable (by other Slovaks, at least) by their particular dialect. One modern urban legend tells of a foreign student from Africa who went to Košice to learn Slovak, but upon taking up studies in Bratislava was surprised to learn that he "couldn't speak Slovak." East Slovaks are held to be among the country's biggest producers (usually homemade) and consumers of *slivovica* (plum brandy) and *borovička* (juniper brandy), and from this region comes the drinking term *kapurkova* ("the gate drink," or parting drink). In general, Slovaks from the east are considered by other Slovaks to be overly emotional—meaning that in addition to drinking more, they fight more, and generally react to situations in a more emotional manner.

Beside being heavy drinkers and fun-loving individuals, Easterners are, on the flipside, positively stereotyped as being ambitious, goal-oriented, and assertive—the proof being their generally heavy representation in government, show business, and executive jobs. Because East Slovakia generally suffers from a lack of investment and a higher unemployment rate, many Easterners relocate to Bratislava and West Slovakia for employment purposes. Thus, some people from Bratislava and the surrounding communities complain that Easterners are taking their jobs, lowering average salaries (because they will work for less than locals), and driving up the cost of real estate.

Slovak Nationalism

Although not an immediately detectable aspect of the Slovak character, nationalism is an underlying sentiment that occasionally creeps into day-to-day conversation. Tensions with ethnic Roma (Gypsies) and Hungarians in Slovakia have been noticeable for many years, and a one-issue political party—Slovenská Národná Strana (the Slovak National Party)—has received a sizeable portion of the vote in national elections (more than the 5 percent threshold to enter parliament, at least in 2006 and 2010) by capitalizing on xenophobic fears that Roma and Hungarians present a threat to Slovak sovereignty. Between 2006 and 2010, the Slovak National Party was a part of the ruling government coalition, and as such was successful in pushing through some controversial policies that were meant to bolster Slovak nationalism. One of these, the Slovak Language Act, passed in 2009, stated that municipalities and public offices could be fined up to €5,000 for not using Slovak, the official state language, properly. This measure was, in reality, a thinly veiled effort to discourage the use of Hungarian, particularly in some southern Slovak villages and towns where Hungarians are a sizeable minority and serve on local town councils.

In the spring of 2010, the Slovak National Party also pushed through parliament a new Patriotism Act, designed to promote the national flag, anthem, and symbols in schools. The law states that the national anthem must be sung every Monday in state primary and secondary schools, and in universities. Classes are also required to display state symbols, the flag, and anthem lyrics, and include other "patriotic education" as part of the curriculum. These measures have met with considerable resistance. As one parent told Agence France-Presse (AFP), "My son will not sing the anthem every Monday. One week he will be sick, next week his bus will be late so that he misses the first Monday lesson." Resistance to the Patriotism Act is based not on disrespect for the flag or anthem, but on the fact that a government law is forcing them to show allegiance. Unlike North Americans, Slovaks are accustomed to singing their anthem only on special occasions.

ATTITUDES TOWARD FOREIGNERS AND MINORITIES

The Slovaks are generally a tolerant people. That said, there are noticeable tensions and discrimination among some Slovaks directed variously at Roma, Hungarians, and homosexuals. Tensions, disagreements, misunderstandings, old stereotypes, and relatively common discrimination against these minorities still persist to varying degrees, even within the political realm. An international study in late 2009, for example, confirmed that 78 percent of Slovaks held unfavorable views of the Roma (within central and eastern Europe, only the Czechs showed more dislike of them). Similarly, more than one in four Slovaks expressed negative attitudes toward Jews, and the same study found that 34 percent of Slovaks perceived Hungary as posing a major threat. (The study also showed that 37 percent of Hungarians perceived Slovakia to be a major threat.)

Any outward expression of homosexuality is still generally not tolerated in Slovakia, although there are some signs that this may be very slowly changing. The Slovak gay, lesbian, and bisexual community attempted to hold a Gay Pride Parade in Bratislava in May 2010, but in the weeks and days leading up to it members of conservative, religious, and skinhead/neo-Nazi groups demonstrated against the event, describing the participants as "perverts" and "deviants," and arguing that homosexuality destroyed traditional family values. On the day of the parade there were more violent and verbally abusive protesters present than supporters—many of whom were probably too frightened to turn up—with few police to keep order despite months of threats on neo-Nazi Web sites. This situation forced the parade organizers to cancel the event out of concern for safety. The anti-gay demonstrations and the lack of preparation by, and apathy of, the police drew criticism from foreign embassies and diplomats representing the USA, Canada, and Britain, among others.

Despite the lingering tensions with Roma and Hungarians, ethnic diversity in Slovakia is growing.

Nowadays one is likely to notice foreign students and other visitors on the streets of most major cities. Unpleasantly loud groups of British men on "stag parties" are noticeable. Bratislava, particularly, is used to a foreign presence and influence, and the language skills of people in the service industry reflect this here more than in other regions.

There is a small Korean population in cities such as Žilina and Piešťany, where Korean manufacturers such as Kia Motors and others have been recently established.

THE VIETNAMESE

In the 1980s the communist Czechoslovak government invited Vietnamese guest workers to the country to labor in Czech and Slovak factories. The Vietnamese authorities encouraged this policy, with the expectation that they would return as skilled workers. (Other reasons included repayment of the Vietnamese war debt, and a labor surplus in Vietnam). Many of the emigrants, however, did not return home. Some did not strictly work in the factories and instead started illegal businesses, trafficking cheap merchandise from Vietnam. There are Vietnamese shopkeepers in almost every sizeable Slovak city, running *Čínske obchody* ("Chinese shops") selling cheap clothing and other goods. Shortly after the Velvet Revolution some of these previously poor migrants became quite rich when they legitimized their businesses. Some became involved in organized crime and in Vietnamese mafia groups in the 1990s. These various factors have contributed to the poor stereotype that many Slovaks hold of Asians in general.

Disabled persons in Slovakia, although not outwardly discriminated against, have a hard time as regards access to services and transportation. Very few businesses, public buildings, buses, or trains have made efforts to accommodate persons with physical challenges, who consequently face considerable inequality and disadvantage in their day-to-day activities and quality of life.

Recent changes to the building code stipulate that new buildings and those under reconstruction must have facilities for the disabled, but as yet few changes have been made regarding disabled access to transportation. Some city buses in large cities have disability access, but certainly not all. Travelers with physical disabilities planning to travel by train are recommended to contact the railway company ahead of time which will then—and only then—provide special access services.

chapter **three**

CUSTOMS & TRADITIONS

The considerable changes that Slovakia has experienced throughout the last century have not necessarily led to a great decline in the practice of older customs and traditions. Although contemporary Slovaks do not live in the same way as their forebears of a hundred years ago—or even as their parents did—and political and social change continues, most remain rooted in the customs and traditions of the past through annual celebrations: Christmas and Easter, regular festivals, family occasions, and folklore. As a people who have long struggled to maintain their distinctive cultural identity in the face of both external and internal forces, they remain proud of their many customs and traditions.

CHRISTMAS AND NEW YEAR

Christmas (Vianoce) is the predominant holiday celebration in Slovakia, and even today the Christian celebration remains linked with the old pagan feast of the winter solstice. (A few pagan myths are still observed by some Slovaks, although these may nowadays be given a Christian twist.) Significant dates associated with Christmas time include the following.

November 11

St. Martin's Day (Svätomartinske dni), the beginning of the winter solstice.

PUBLIC HOLIDAYS	
January 1	Deň vzniku Slovenskej republiky (Establishment of the Slovak Republic)
January 6	Traja králi (Three Kings Day)
March/April	Veľkonočný piatok (Good Friday)
March/April	Veľkonočný pondelok (Easter Monday)
May 1	Sviatok práce (International Workers' Day)
May 8	Deň víťazstva nad fašizmom (Day of Victory Over Fascism)
July 5	Sviatok svätého Cyrila a Metoda (Saints Cyril and Methodius Day)
August 29	Výročie Slovenského národného povstania (SNP Day)
September 1	Deň Ústavy Slovenskej republiky (Constitution Day)
September 15	Sviatok Panny Márie Sedembolestnej (Day of the Blessed Virgin Mary)
November 1	Sviatok všetkých svätých (All Saints' Day)
November 17	Deň boja za slobodu a demokraciu (Struggle for Freedom and Democracy Day)
December 24	Štedrý večer, or Štedrý deň (Christmas Eve)
December 25	Prvý sviatok vianočný (Christmas Day)
December 26	Druhý sviatok vianočný (Second Christmas Holiday)

November 30

On St. Andrew's Day, *halušky* (the national dish of potato dumplings, similar to Italian *gnocchi*) are made. Traditionally, an unmarried girl would put slips of paper bearing the names of young men into the *halušky* while they are boiled in water; the first name to float to the surface would be that of her future husband.

December 6

On St. Nicholas's Day (Deň Svätého Mikuláša) Slovaks traditionally exchanged gifts. Some people still observe this day with small presents, but most now have their main present-opening celebration on Christmas Eve. Traditionally, on the eve of St. Nicholas's Day, children would leave their shoes or boots on the windowsill; in the morning the good children would find theirs filled with little treats, usually fruit and nuts, and the naughty ones would find coal. In some villages the day is still observed by boys dressing up as Sv. Mikuláš and his entourage—an angel and a devil—who visit families with very small children. The little children are supposed to say an improvised prayer (usually humorous) and in exchange receive fruit and nuts from the "angel." Those who misbehave get coal, or in some cases potatoes, from the "devil."

December 24

Christmas Eve (Štedrý večer, literally, "bountiful eve", or Štedrý deň). The "bounty" comes in the form of a wide range of festive foods, which tradition says should include twelve different dishes on this day. Although not every Slovak household will now provide twelve dishes, many will come close to this number, still including garlic on the table as a means of warding off bad spirits, honey to bring good health, along with wafers, nuts, cooked peas or beans, and dried fruit. Other Christmas dishes include cabbage soup—to which Protestants may also add smoked meats and sausage—and *opekance*, small pieces of sweet dough with poppy seeds, symbolizing wealth, and also known as *bobaľky* or *pupáčky*. Nowadays, fish (usually carp) is the most commonly served main course at Christmas meals, with potato salad, particularly among Catholics. The fish scales are said to bring wealth into the house; fish soup is also common.

As so many dishes belong to the Christmas Eve celebrations, they are normally served as several courses. The usual starter is *prípitok*, a shot of liquor, normally involving a toast; then Christmas wafers (*oblátky*) with garlic and honey; these are followed by the *opekance*; then soup; and then the main meal.

Preparations in most households start early in Advent with the purchasing of nuts, poppy seeds, flour, and other necessary items. Then, for several days before Christmas, Slovak women are baking and cleaning—Slovak tradition

also says that the house must be cleaned before Christmas Eve. The family will normally fast all day on Christmas Eve and have the meal at supper time, though customs vary from family to family. The devout go to midnight mass—by far the best-attended church service of the year.

In most Slovak families, presents are opened after the Christmas Eve meal. The parcels are put under a decorated tree, and today most young children are told that Ježiško (Baby Jesus) has brought them, but some families still keep up the tradition of Santa Claus's Slovak counterpart, Dedo Mráz (Father Frost). Slovaks do not generally give and receive a great number of gifts; Christmas has not yet been commercialized to the degree it has in the West.

Leading up to Christmas, town squares are decorated with lights and dressed trees. For the foreign visitor, the Christmas markets may be the most charming and memorable part of the Christmas season in Slovakia. For several weeks beforehand these attractive markets sell traditional crafts, gifts, clothing, and festive food and drink. Every evening, regardless of the weather, the town centers bustle with people and good cheer, with everyone enjoying whatever is on offer. Traditionally available—and great favorites—are *ciganska pecienka* (fried pork or chicken with onions and mustard on a bun), *loksa* (made from wheat flour with various fillings, including garlic, goose liver, poppy seeds, nuts, or chocolate), *varene vino* (mulled wine), and in some regions, *medovina* (warm honey wine). The best-known of these Christmas markets is the one in Bratislava, which spreads over two squares—Hlavné námestie and Františkánske námestie.

Christmas Day and December 26 are normally spent visiting relatives and simply enjoying the atmosphere of Christmas. Some people attend church services or visit the "Betlehems" (nativity scenes) that are displayed in churches and many town squares.

December 31
New Year's Eve, or Silvester, is named for the pope St. Sylvester, who died on this day in 335. The evening is normally spent attending special dances, gathering on the town square to make a toast, or just watching the celebrations on TV. Midnight (and even earlier) sees a great explosion of fireworks, both officially endorsed by the towns and put on by private individuals. Drinking and fireworks normally continue well into the early morning.

Christmas and New Year Greetings
Slovaks wish each other "*Veselé vianoce a Štastný nový rok*"—"A Merry Christmas and a Happy New Year."

FAŠIANGY (CARNIVAL)
From December 26 until the beginning of Lent, forty days before Easter, is the period Slovaks refer to as Fašiangy

(Carnival). Originating as a Catholic tradition, Fašiangy is nowadays characterized in Slovakia by multiple balls, held by cities, towns, villages, schools, and other institutions.

In some villages the old traditional Fašiangy celebrations are still practiced. These are normally held from the last Sunday before Lent until Tuesday at midnight, and are major theatrical events. They include costumed and masked youths walking from house to house playing music and singing. The songs are normally addressed specifically to the unmarried girls of the household, and the entertaining visitors are typically offered *slanina* (smoked bacon) and other treats that will be prohibited during Lent. As is the case with many Slovak celebrations, consuming large amounts of food and hard drink go hand-in-hand with Fašiangy customs: *medovina*, *bravčová huspenina* (pork jelly), and fried *šišky* or *pampúchy* (filled pastries) are typical. On Fat (Shrove) Tuesday, the day before Ash Wednesday (the beginning of Lent), the end of Fašiangy is marked by burying a contrabass (double bass) to symbolize the end of the festivities.

EASTER

Easter celebrations, as in many countries, begin on Holy Thursday for Christians in Slovakia, and Good Friday is a state holiday. While most people don't work on Good Friday, most stores and supermarkets are open for the all-important grocery shopping. The women of the family get busy with cooking meat and baked goods, making other preparations for the meal, and cleaning the home. A typical Easter Monday meal consists of potato salad with mayonnaise, cooked ham, cold cuts, and sandwiches. The women are also expected to prepare the traditional decorative Easter eggs (*kraslice*), which are blown, then dyed and/or hand painted with intricate patterns.

On Easter Monday (variously called Šibačka, Polievačka, or Oblievačka) there is a particularly Slovak custom. In the past, boys and men would visit their close female friends and/or family members, starting early and waking the girls by pouring buckets of water over their heads and gently striking them on the legs with a bunch of long, thin twigs or switches made from willow, birch, or decorated branches (called *korbáč*). The splashing and whipping were thought to keep women fertile, healthy, and pure for the rest of the year. The *korbáč* were handwoven and decorated with colorful ribbons. It is said that the ribbons were added by each victim in turn, testifying to the number of girls the boy managed to soak and/or whip. This went on throughout the day.

The custom is now rarely followed, at least in urban areas, but in some places continues, maybe in a milder form: the bucket of water is replaced by a spray of perfume, a small cup of water, or a quick squirt from a water pistol. In return for this attention, the girls are expected to give the boys some small change or painted or chocolate eggs; adult men are offered a drink of spirits (alcohol is a big part of all Slovak celebrations). Tradition says that if an unmarried girl is not targeted for such activities she is considered unattractive and unmarriageable, but few now take such suggestions seriously. In those villages where the old tradition continues, men and boys may be on horseback with their rattles and braided *korbáč*, perhaps dressed in traditional folk costumes, singing, and playing the accordion. As might be expected, the tradition is dear to men, and often dreaded by women, some of whom have to change their clothes several times a day after multiple soakings, and many of whom have been working hard over the previous two days, shopping and preparing food for the Easter meal. The Slovak journalist Martina Pisárová remarks, "Never in my life have I met a woman who would praise this tradition." The men, however, say that women only pretend not to like it, but secretly enjoy being the center of attention.

NAME DAYS AND BIRTHDAYS

In the Slovak calendar each day of the year has at least one personal name assigned to it, based on the Roman Catholic calendar of saints. Slovaks therefore celebrate their name day (*meniny* or *sviatok*)—the date corresponding to their own given name. Name days are accorded as much importance as a person's birthday, thus children are normally given names that are assigned a date—for who would want their child to miss out on the opportunity to have an extra celebration?

Name day and birthday celebrations are common not only at home among family and friends, but also in the workplace and at school. The celebrant will normally give candies (to his or her classmates, for example) or a shot of alcohol (sometimes at work). Close friends and coworkers will usually give the celebrant a small gift, such as flowers or something sweet, and wish the person "*Všetko najlepšie*" ("All the best!") with a formal handshake and/or a kiss on both cheeks accompanied by a short speech. To the unschooled foreigner, such exchanges may appear rather formal. Rarely will a Slovak simply say "Happy birthday" (*Všetko najlepšie k narodeninám)* or name day in passing.

So entrenched are the saints' name days in the Slovak psyche that they are commonly referred to in Slovak proverbs—in fact, there are probably as many proverbs involving names as there are name days (that is, at least one for each day of the year).

Although in days gone by the Catholic Church promoted the celebration of name days over birthdays—because the latter were seen as a pagan tradition—Slovaks today celebrate both with equal vigor. When a name day or birthday celebrant hosts a party in a restaurant, the expectation is that the celebrant will pay the bill. The guests naturally bring a small gift, but the party costs are the responsibility of the celebrant—in contrast to what happens in many other countries, where it is friends or family who may host a meal on the celebrant's behalf.

SATURDAY WEDDINGS

Weddings in Slovakia are, almost without exception, held on Saturdays. As with most Slovak celebrations tradition tends to rule the day, and there are several unique elements.

On the morning of the ceremony the groom normally visits the bride at her parents' house. This traditionally involves a speech delivered on the groom's behalf by an elderly male family member or friend (the *starejší*), asking the bride's parents for her hand. In response, the parents give the couple their blessing, and the bride and groom then normally go straight off to a wedding photo shoot, when both parties are looking their best. Then may follow a pre-wedding ceremony, sometimes conducted by a traditionally costumed master of ceremonies, and the first feast of the day, with a speech by the bride in which she sincerely thanks her parents for raising her.

Slivovica Wedding Bribes

There are many family and regional traditions practiced at Slovak weddings, but one charming custom was the act of offering *slivovica* (plum brandy) as a bribe to local farmers who obstructed the bride and groom on their way to or from the church or town hall. Tradition had it that a young girl gathered the plums to make the brandy for her future wedding, or their fathers made the brandy shortly after the birth of a daughter, to be put aside for this day. The custom continues in its modern version, when local men stop the decorated bridal cars, and receive some *slivovica* or small change in return for their congratulations.

The church or civil ceremony is normally the shortest and least eventful part of the day, lasting usually only about an hour. Don't imagine that the celebrations are now half over! On the contrary, they have only just begun. After the ceremony, the newlyweds greet their guests one by one and receive their congratulations, and sometimes flowers, then make their way to the reception venue, where the guests have gathered, sometimes accompanied by a Roma band. Now a plate-breaking ceremony (*rozbíjanie taniera*) takes place, which involves the shattering of a plate on the ground to bring good luck. The bride and groom must sweep up the shards. Some guests have fun at this point, and kick the pieces around to make it more difficult, but the bride has to be extra careful—any leftover shards, tradition says, symbolize the children her husband will have with another woman.

Then a meal will be served. The first course involves another tradition: the bride and groom feed each other with soup from one bowl, with one spoon, symbolizing the necessary sharing and caring of married life. Throughout the long evening of eating and dancing that follows, guests regularly tap their glasses as a signal for the newlyweds to kiss. There may also be regular choruses of "Živio," a Russian song wishing long life to, and toasting, the couple.

Wedding parties normally continue well into the early hours. There are traditional dances—*nevestinský tanec* ("the bridal dance"), *metlový tanec* ("the broom dance"), and *začepčenie* ("the taking of the veil"), which involve the bride in some wardrobe changes. The bridal dance involves each male guest dancing with the bride, and each female guest with the groom, usually in exchange for a little money. As more money is added to the pot, the music gets faster. The money goes to the couple to set up their home. The broom dance includes an extra man, who takes a broom as his partner. When the music stops he drops the broom and everyone quickly changes partners; whoever is left without one must dance with the broom.

Začepčenie is an old tradition whereby the new wife removed the wreath that she had been wearing on her head throughout the ceremony and reception, and replaced it with a colorful traditional bonnet. The delicate wreath represented purity and virginity, and the bonnet marked her transition from girlhood to womanhood. While the wreath was removed, the older women guests would sing songs. Nowadays this tradition normally involves the bride's veil being removed by local women wearing traditional costumes, accompanied by the *starejší* acting as the groom's representative. The *starejší* is asked questions by the women—normally of a tricky and humorous variety—and once all the questions have been answered the bride's veil is placed on another girl's head, as a sign that she will be married in the following year. The modern version of this tradition may also involve the bride removing the flower from the groom's buttonhole and standing on it, meaning that he will not find another woman. At the close of this little ceremony the bride may change into another dress, as a further mark of her transition to wife.

Some Slovak weddings also involve a symbolic "kidnapping" of the bride at a moment when the groom is seemingly not keeping a close eye on his new wife at the reception. The young male guests steal the bride away to a local pub, where they drink beer, champagne, or the harder stuff until the groom finds them. The groom is then expected to pay the bill—an incentive to rescue his bride quickly, which may be a hard task in a large city.

SLOVAK FOLK CULTURE

Smiling women in long skirts and bonnets, dancing with colorfully dressed men, and folk music, with evocative laments, expressions of love, and moments of despair and triumph—such images feature prominently in most publicity aimed at tourists, and while these might sound like fragments of the past, or just putting on a show for visitors, such displays are in fact a common element of modern Slovak custom.

Slovakia's rural way of life remained largely unbroken until well into the twentieth century, and still continues in

some regions. Its varied folk culture is alive and well, even among the young, and this is in large part thanks to the communist government, which strongly promoted the celebration of folklore as an important element of socialist society. Folk culture was encouraged as a means of ensuring the people would keep an interest in their own arts, music, and dance, rather than adopt a cosmopolitan-style admiration of the cultures and arts of other countries and societies. With this in mind, early communist governments sponsored the creation of professional folk groups, such as Slovenský ľudový umelecký kolektív, or SĽUK (Slovak Folk Art Association) and Lúčnica, the Slovak National Folklore Ballet, and numerous smaller groups were established locally.

Slovak folk costumes, dances, and music reflect the diversity of influences the region has seen throughout its history—Celtic, Roman, Hungarian, Slavic, and German. Numerous festivals between July and September celebrate the rich traditions with music, crafts, and food, and these are not merely for the old—Slovak and foreign tourists of all ages come out in huge numbers to take part. Slovakia's most famous folk festival, Folklórny festival Východná, which has taken place in the village of Východná in Middle Slovakia every July for almost sixty years, nowadays features the best troupes from Slovakia and also international performers. Before 1989, this festival was staged not only as a celebration of Slovak folklore, but also as a clever distraction from Catholicism—it used to be held on the same weekend as the most important annual pilgrimage from Levoča to Mariánska hora. Nowadays Folklórny festival Východná is a multiday event, recorded and broadcast on national television.

Similar folk festivals take place throughout the country all summer long and well into the month of September. Several cities and towns host an annual *jarmok* (fair) highlighting folk traditions in early September, for example. These fairs normally include staged events and booths where artisans sell their handmade crafts and wares. The most famous of these, Radvanský jarmok in Banská Bystrica, is known as the "fair of all fairs," and tradition has it that Slovakia's best known bandit, Juraj Jánošík, used to visit it. Held in Banská Bystrica's picturesque old center, Radvanský jarmok is accompanied by presentations of folklore ensembles, music groups, competitions, merry-go-rounds, and tasting of the year's first *burčiak* (young wine, or the stage between must and wine). A close second in importance, and similar in presentation, is Tradičný trnavský jarmok, held annually in Trnava.

Juraj Jánošík, the Slovak Robin Hood

Few foreigners leave Slovakia without having heard of the nation's most famous outlaw, Juraj Jánošík (c. 1688–1713) who, according to tradition, robbed the rich and gave to the poor. A modern-day symbol of resistance, and immortalized in song, poetry, prose, and film, he became known also in Poland and the Czech Republic. His legend was shaped by Slovak activists and writers in the nineteenth century, and his image was reinforced when poems about him later became part of the Slovak and Czech school literature curricula. During the anti-Nazi Slovak National Uprising, one of the partisan groups famously bore his name.

While legend often trumps historical fact, what is certain about Jánošík is that he was born and grew up in the village of Terchová in the present-day district of Žilina, in northwestern Slovakia. As a young prison guard in 1710, he helped a prisoner to escape and together they formed a forest robber group, which Jánošík led. Most of their victims were rich merchants, and the group was reportedly exceptionally chivalrous, killing none of their victims and even helping an accidentally injured priest. Jánošík was captured and executed for his thievery in spring 1713.

chapter **four**

MAKING FRIENDS

Friends and relations are of great importance to Slovaks, and they and their concerns normally take precedence over everything else. Under communist rule, no one else could be trusted, and friendship is still taken very seriously. False friends among Slovaks are rare. Friendships forged early in life—normally through school, neighborhood, or early work relations—are particularly firm, tending to last well into adulthood and even old age.

Whereas North Americans may be accustomed to meeting someone and then describing that person as a friend, in Slovakia this is rarely the case. For Slovaks, such a person is an acquaintance, and friendships take longer to develop. Similarly, native English speakers are normally comfortable with using first names, or even nicknames, in addressing people they have just met or with whom they are engaged in business. Slovaks, in most cases, will be uncomfortable with such informality and the visitor is advised to let them take the initiative in using first names.

This said, however, foreigners don't normally have difficulty meeting Slovaks, who are a highly sociable, warm, and hospitable people. English speakers in particular should have little problem making new acquaintances, who in time may become good friends. Probably the easiest way is to go to a pub—and this does not mean you have to drink alcohol. While Slovaks

consume a lot of beer, they also frequent pubs for other reasons. A pint of Kofola (cola) is probably just as normal a drink among pub goers as beer. Pub culture in Slovakia embraces young and old, and although retired men may go to pubs more often and in greater numbers than other segments of the population, they tend to have their own haunts.

Slovaks are normally punctual, and stick to their word as regards meetings and arrangements between friends. It rarely happens that a Slovak fails to show up for a planned meeting, for example. In the event that plans change, you'll be told in good time.

MAKING CONVERSATION

If you are able to talk about your own interests—whether business, hobbies, family, or otherwise—you may be surprised at how quickly you'll feel accepted by new Slovak acquaintances. As many Slovaks, for professional or travel reasons, are looking for interesting ways to improve their language skills, English-speaking guests who demonstrate openness and sociability are likely to be made welcome. Slovaks like to hear about their visitors' own lives, so if you have photos of your family, friends and home, these will go a long way to humanizing you as a foreign visitor. It's generally safe to ask them about their own hobbies, family, or work. At the very least, these topics are good icebreakers, and you can move on to other subjects once you've found some common ground. Generally speaking, demonstrating a great deal of self-confidence is not considered a virtue; Slovaks tend to prefer modesty as a quality in their friends.

As we have seen, Slovaks tend to be critical of the political, economic, and social situation in their country, so, if you dare, these are also good topics—but be prepared for the conversation to take a negative or complaining tone if you probe too deeply. To keep things positive, ask for some recommendations of places to visit. Most Slovaks tend to be quite opinionated about the "best" tourist sites, and generally showing an interest in their culture and what it has to offer will quickly win you points.

FRIENDLY RELATIONS

Outward displays of affection between good friends, regardless of gender, are a normal sight, signaling the degrees of warmth and openness that are common traits among Slovaks. Friends meet with a double kiss or a handshake, and sometimes a hug. Girls and young women often hold hands in the street—just good friends, sisters, or cousins.

Warm relationships, although not necessarily friendships, are the norm among neighbors, work colleagues, and others met on a regular basis. A friendly "*Dobrý den*" ("good day") or "*Dobrý večer*" ("Good

evening") upon meeting an acquaintance is the norm, and is generally expected, as is the friendly utterance of "*Dovidenia*" ("till I see you again") upon departure. Such greetings are usual even between neighbors or colleagues who are not on the best of terms, and are also extended to complete strangers in public elevators, train compartments, or small shops, for example. Similarly, when Slovaks ask a friend or acquaintance "*Ako sa máš?*" ("How are you?") they generally mean it. In other words, it is not simply used as a greeting, as is often the case elsewhere, and the response will be a genuine expression of how the person feels—sometimes in considerable detail.

Warm relations between acquaintances and friends, and general cordiality, reflect the system of connections in Slovakia. "Who you know" is an important element in Slovak society—particularly because such relations might lead to spending less, avoiding red tape, securing employment, and finding favors in general. Connections were absolutely essential to navigating the communist regime, and remain an important and palpable part of Slovak society today. Learning to negotiate the economic, social, and political system through one's family, friends, and friendly acquaintances can apparently go a long way to determining one's fate in life.

FORMALITY

As noted in Chapter 2, hierarchies and titles are reflected in the way Slovaks address each other. Such formality should not be overlooked, as any indiscretion can seem rude, unfriendly, or plain disrespectful. A good way to gauge when you've changed from being an acquaintance to a friend is to take note of when formalities with contacts begin to loosen.

Greetings are important. When entering a small or medium-sized shop, or when using the elevator in a block of apartments, be sure to acknowledge the shopkeeper or your fellow elevator riders. In small places it is still the custom to greet even strangers as you pass them—silence in such circumstances is considered rude. You may feel this is just empty politeness, but Slovaks attach considerable meaning to it.

Note that "Good morning" should not be used after 8:00 a.m. Visitors who are accustomed to wishing someone a good morning until noon will meet with a different response.

OPENNESS AND DIRECTNESS

Simply put, the Slovaks are an open and direct people. Usually coming straight to the point in business negotiations and in regular day-to-day interactions, they waste little time in expressing themselves. A foreigner, who out of politeness uses phrases like "maybe" or "perhaps," will generally be seen as lacking in purpose. Visitors will find themselves much better understood if they simply get to the point. As long as one is gracious about it, skipping

COMMON SLOVAK GREETINGS (POZDRAVY)
Ahoj (an informal multipurpose greeting) "Hello" or "Good-bye"
Ahojte (informal) "Hello" or "Good-bye" to two or more persons
Servus (informal) "Hello" or "Good-bye"
Dobré ráno (formal) "Good morning" (used until 8:00 a.m. only)
Dobrý deň (formal) "Good day" (used after 8:00 a.m. until dusk)
Dobrý večer (formal) "Good evening" (used only on meeting, not when saying good-bye)
Dobrú noc (formal or informal) "Good night." Formally used only upon departure; informally used when going to bed
Dovidenia (formal) "Till I see you again" or "good-bye"
Čau (informal) "Hello" or "Good-bye"
Zbohom (formal/informal) "Farewell" (said when you won't meet again for a long time)

the small talk and cutting to the chase is not normally regarded as impolite.

HOSPITALITY

To English-speaking foreigners, Slovaks can be incredibly generous in their hospitality. This may welcome social interaction with you as a relaxed and convenient means of practicing their English-language skills.

Invitations

Among close relations it is common to be invited for a *pivo* (beer) or two at a local pub or restaurant. Such invitations are particularly common among male friends. Unusual for many Westerners will be that the person doing the inviting is expected to pay. Offers to contribute to the bill are not insulting, but are likely to be firmly refused.

To be invited to visit a Slovak at home is a sign of authentic friendship. English-speaking foreigners are almost always treated with the utmost hospitality, warm handshakes, and broad smiles. Many Slovaks do not live in family houses, but rather in apartments. From the outside, apartment blocks (*paneláky*) are the most visible reminder of the not-so-distant communist past: their architecture clearly stresses function over form, though in recent years the uniformly two-tone gray exteriors have begun to be colorfully painted. Stairwells and elevators are commonly maintained by the owner of the building. Don't be put off by a dark and dingy appearance—once you are inside an individual apartment, the situation normally improves in terms of aesthetics. People generally own their apartments, so interior decor can vary considerably, and rooms may be anything from small boxes with old, simple furniture to a more open space with a modern style. If you are invited to a family house, you can expect a more luxurious experience, as ownership of a house is generally a sign of upper/middle class status—or at least a lucky inheritance.

It is customary for an invited guest to bring the host a small present. A bottle of wine or a modest dessert would be suitable.

Punctuality is valued among Slovaks, and this is particularly true of invitations. They will prepare quite elaborate meals with at least three courses (soup, main course, and dessert) for their guests, and if you arrive late something could very well be spoiled or wasted.

Taking your shoes off is expected, particularly when you visit an apartment—less so when you visit a house. Your host may tell you to leave your shoes on, out of politeness, but you should still take them off and leave them at the door. Your shoes should be polished and in decent condition. You will be offered slippers.

In their homes, Slovaks are very hospitable, and you will be offered a meal, or at the very least snacks with drinks. The drink will probably be alcohol, such as *slivovica* (plum brandy) or *borovička* (juniper brandy, with a ginlike flavor), which is sometimes homemade, particularly if your hosts have a garden. The general rule is that these offerings should not be refused, which would be considered impolite, so if you are a nondrinker do take a sip, or politely explain that you cannot drink alcohol—perhaps for medical reasons. If a small cake or bottle of alcohol is offered, take it, as it is expected that a guest should accept such gifts.

Your glass and plate will rarely be empty in a Slovak home. Lunch is the main meal of the day, so you will eat well if invited at this time, particularly on a Sunday. Finishing what's in your glass or on your plate signals a wish for another helping—so get used to the idea of leaving something if you don't want any more. It is polite to refuse when first asked, but you will be asked again, at which time you accept.

Reciprocating an invitation is not expected, but is certainly appreciated. For a visitor, inviting Slovak friends out to a restaurant after they have hosted you in their home is appropriate.

NAMES AND NICKNAMES

Compared to English, the range of names in use in Slovakia may seem quite small. There are certain names that you are bound to hear again and again—for example, Jana, Martin, Ján, Miro, Katarína, Veronika, and Zuzana.

There are few unusual names. Although parents can technically choose any name they like, if what they have chosen is not a recognized name a birth registration clerk has the power to refuse it, in the best interests of the child. The use of middle names is rare, so there can be several people with the same name and surname—which makes finding a Slovak friend on Facebook, for example, a potential challenge.

However, as change is a constant, in recent years it has become fashionable for Slovak parents to choose foreign names, and middle names are beginning to occur as well.

There are two common elements in Slovak names—slav (glory) and mir (great, famous, or peace). Many names are compound names formed from Slavonic elements such as these—for example, Miroslav, Vladimir, or Jaroslava. The stress, as with all Slovak words, is placed on the first syllable.

Women's surnames in Slovakia generally end with –ová or -ská. The Slovak language deems this grammatically necessary when talking about women or girls. Foreign female visitors may therefore find that their own name is given the Slovak treatment—Karen Smith, for example, may become pani Smithová (if she is married, or slečna Smithová if she is not), particularly in a formal situation. Foreign names and celebrities in the media are sometimes given similar treatment—Céline Dionová, Kelly Clarksonová, or Serena Williamsová, for example.

Among friends and family, Slovaks will commonly make a kind of nickname, pet name, or term of endearment out of a first name, formed by adding a new ending. For example, if a person's name is Peter, he may be called Petrík or Peťo, which can mean many things—"little Peter" (used as a term of endearment to a child), "Pete," "Peter, my buddy," and so on.

ROMANCING THE FOREIGNER

Slovaks today travel much more than they used to, and the sight of foreigners in Slovakia is far from rare, so the single visitor is not likely to be viewed as exotic here. Nonetheless, foreigners deemed eligible, and who approach their Slovak counterparts in an open and warm manner, have a fair chance of being paired off. Most young Slovaks will have had some interaction with a foreign guest—whether through school, work, or vacations—and everyone knows someone who has dated a foreigner. However, don't think that young, single Slovaks are on the hunt for a "rich foreigner." The old stereotype of the poor, deprived young woman (or man, but most often a woman) desperately seeking to escape communism is long outdated. Young Slovaks today have little desire or reason to "escape" their country, and a foreign love interest certainly wouldn't be necessary to do so.

Young people tend to be relaxed about such formalities, but if you are male, and you have a date, bring flowers. Although Slovak women do not now expect such gifts—particularly from foreign men—the gesture will be warmly appreciated. More impressive will be knowing that you should present an odd number of flowers, as according to tradition an even-numbered bouquet is for funerals. If the flowers are wrapped in paper, take it off before you present them.

It's worth noting that what could be considered sexual harassment in many Western countries (leering, wandering fingers, propositioning, and the like) passes as "natural male behavior" in Slovakia. Foreign women are not likely to encounter this, as Slovak men tend to be better behaved around them. Similarly, dates between teachers and students are not frowned upon here as they are elsewhere. While in the USA or UK a student–teacher relationship is likely to spell the end of the teacher's professional career, in Slovakia few see this as wrong. As long as the student is of legal age (above fifteen), such relationships rarely raise an eyebrow.

chapter five

THE SLOVAKS AT HOME

What may seem like hardships to a North American or Western European—a lack of air-conditioning, no car or only one car per family, and a small living space—is of little consequence to most Slovaks. This is simply the everyday reality for many people who live in apartment blocks, and for whom the idea of owning a house is a distant dream. While more people are now building their own homes, the sheer number of apartment blocks in the cities and towns attests to the majority who don't. In part because of such living conditions and in part because Slovaks are generally an active bunch, many people simply don't spend much time at home, which for them is merely a place to sleep. During the week they are at work, or running errands and/or socializing in town, and on weekends they are always out and about—particularly those who live in apartment blocks without a backyard.

HOUSING

Most Slovaks, at some point in their lives, have lived in an apartment block (*panelák*). To most Westerners, these buildings seem cramped, architecturally uninspired (horrid versions of Functionalism), and lacking in privacy. In some cases, as many as four or five people will live in what is technically a two-bedroom apartment, with some rooms

serving multiple functions (bedroom by night, living room by day). The heating and water supply are normally centrally controlled, meaning that individuals have no control over the temperature, except by opening or closing windows, and the water supply can dry up with little warning—particularly during the summer months, when pipelines and systems are frequently repaired. These *paneláky* were built in many Eastern Bloc countries and served not only as a cheap source of housing, but were intended to integrate home, work, and social life, often with schools, factories, clinics, and cultural centers nearby. In communist times, urbanization and industrialization policies that drove people from the countryside collectively into towns and cities (and public housing estates) took away individual responsibility for actively designing or caring for one's space. Since 1989, there has been some variety in the architecture and design of apartment-style housing, and the *paneláky* have been joined by a more diverse range of apartment complexes, especially in big towns and cities.

Living in close quarters can lead to the occasional difference with neighbors over noise or what may be perceived as bad behavior. This is particularly true when

the neighbor in question is of a different generation. Many elderly Slovaks live alone in their apartments, and often have little income and nowhere else to go. They will sometimes spend their days on their balconies or in the small courtyards in front of or behind most buildings, and this gives them plenty of opportunity to observe and criticize the behavior of others, sometimes resulting in petty conflicts. Recently young people have begun to rent apartments in groups of four or five (rather than staying at home with their parents until marriage, as was common in the past), and because young Slovaks tend to express their freedom more liberally today in ways such as inviting friends to visit, including those of the opposite gender, this further fuels the fire of gossip, criticism, and hostility.

Those fortunate enough to live in a detached family home, through either inheritance or economic success since 1989, have a greater sense of personal involvement in planning and caring for their space. Thus, such homes will vary greatly, despite normally small tracts of land—which will nevertheless be well used in terms of gardening and growing fruits and vegetables. However, there is one constant—the fence. Visitors may notice that Slovak houses are surrounded, usually right up to the road and/or sidewalk, by solid fences, with a gate. Front yards and driveways that are open and accessible to visitors and passersby don't exist in Slovakia in either city or village settings. If they did, a homeowner would be sure to experience theft and/or vandalism, usually in the form of graffiti.

FAMILY LIFE

"Although research shows that 89 percent of Slovaks still place priority on the family, when it comes to launching their own, they hesitate."
PhDr. Bernardína Bodnárová, Bratislava International Center for Family Studies, June 2002

During communism, when Slovakia was isolated and people could not travel much, the family was a very important part of Slovak life. In the times before communism, the Catholic Church had a big influence on the structure of the family, and in rural Slovak society the family was an important element of survival. Even today family values tend to remain stronger in Slovakia than in Western Europe, for example.

Before the 1989 Velvet Revolution, the law guaranteed individuals a job the day after they finished school, so financial security was more certain, and marriage and starting a family early was the norm. Since then, however, the changing economy and an almost 20 percent unemployment rate at times have discouraged this. Many young Slovaks now choose to travel or work abroad for a while instead.

Until very recently, young adults would normally live at home with their parents until they married, and this is still not unusual. Although most of them will have graduated from school and have a job, staying at home to help with costs or to save money is not considered a step in the wrong direction, as it is in North America, for example. In recent years, however, young people have begun to move out—this reflects changing work opportunities, but also external cultural influences. When Slovaks tended to marry quite young, staying at home until marriage was no great hardship. In communist times, when everyone had an opportunity to work and get an apartment at minimal costs, the norm was to finish school, get married, work, and start having a family. In the 1970s, couples on average married after only three months' acquaintance, the woman was usually pregnant by the age of twenty-two, and 100,000 babies were born a year—a baby boom. Now barely 50,000 babies a year are born (although there was a mini baby boom when those born in the '70s began to have children of their own).

Many young people now leave home for study or work in Bratislava, for example—particularly those from Middle and East Slovakia—and rent apartments with coworkers or friends. Without the guaranteed jobs and cheap homes of the past, couples delay marriage until they can afford their own place (normally a small apartment), and the average age at which the first child is born is rising. Young people today, more so than even a few years ago, consider education and work more important than marriage and babies—a clear reflection of the current financial challenges to be overcome.

Regardless of these changing dynamics, family connections remain very tight, and most people's loyalties remain to their family first, and all others second. Although young people may no longer live at home until they marry, many still contribute financially to their parents' living costs, and because Slovakia is a relatively small country, it is easy to return for regular visits.

With retirement age defined as fifty-three to fifty-seven for women (depending on how many children they have), and sixty for men, elderly people are now the most rapidly growing segment of the Slovak population. Elderly parents or grandparents living with or near younger family members is a tradition still practiced here, although as the economy has changed over the last twenty years, so too has this situation—nursing homes and long-term care facilities, although still rare, are a developing social trend. Similarly, grandparent culture has changed quite dramatically. Thirty or forty years ago, people became grandparents at the age of forty-five, on average, and saw their main role in life as caring for their grandchildren. Now families may be scattered and children older before they start having their own children; thus, grandparents too are older, and the generation gap widens. With fewer grandchildren to care for, and very low pensions, the elderly in Slovakia are increasingly isolated, in poverty, and expecting to live longer. Depression rates are a growing concern among this segment of the population.

Children

Slovak families today tend to have one or two children, and as mentioned above, the average age of first-time parents has been rising as education and other circumstances have changed. The number of children in a family has fallen dramatically over the last thirty to forty years, with an average of 3.04 children per mother in 1960 to 1.32 in 2008.

As the day-to-day working lives of Slovak parents have changed, so too have the day-to-day lives of their children. Recent studies seem to support the general consensus among Slovaks that children today are less disciplined, more hyperactive, and more spoiled than in past generations. Their leisure time is mainly spent on the computer, listening to music, watching television, and hanging out with peers. Some children are active in some types of manual occupation such as handicrafts, home improvement, or leisure gardening, but after-school jobs are a rarity here. Studies show that only 15 percent of Slovak children are regularly, and 35 percent are occasionally, engaged in hobbies. Among adolescents hobbies are even more rare, with most preferring to spend time alone or with friends. Almost half of Slovak children and youth (48.4 percent) are engaged in no leisure activities and most spend as much time chatting with friends, telephoning, or sending text messages as they do reading, completing homework, or searching out information. Similar studies have shown that the rate of participation among young people in the social and political lives of Slovak society has been falling for several years.

Of course, such trends are hardly unique to Slovakia, and what they ultimately mean for the future of Slovak society and culture is open to speculation. Children remain highly prized in Slovak society, and the education, work, and travel possibilities for youth today are altogether different from those prior to 1989. As many Slovaks spend a lot of time outside the home, it is common to see children playing in the streets and in the parks, and young parents pushing baby carriages. An unfortunate reality related to the time Slovaks spend out of doors is that parents are often seen assisting their small children (up to the age of six of seven) to urinate in grassy areas, taking little care do to so discreetly. Public toilets are not uncommon, and most

charge a small fee for use, but Slovak parents say that this is an issue of time, not money.

EDUCATION

The basic school system in Slovakia is composed of preschools (kindergartens; children aged three to six), primary or elementary schools (first stage, aged six to ten; second stage, aged ten to fifteen), secondary schools (consisting of secondary grammar schools, vocational schools, professional training colleges, and conservatories; aged fifteen to nineteen), and higher education institutions (universities; students aged from nineteen).

Schools in Slovakia may be funded by the government, churches, or privately, and in recent years the number of private schools has risen dramatically. School attendance is compulsory for ten years, or until the child is sixteen years of age. Primary and secondary students attend school five days a week from the beginning of September until the end of June. Primary and secondary students normally attend around six classes per day. Second-language instruction nowadays begins as early as kindergarten, with specialized English-language preschools being quite common, particularly in the larger centers. Teaching is a very poorly paid profession in Slovakia; there is a general lack of highly qualified teachers below the university level, and universities are often unable to provide sufficient pay to keep or attract top-quality experts and motivated teachers.

Primary and Secondary Schools

Primary school (*škola*) education is normally preceded by kindergarten, where children may spend up to four years. Most children start primary school in the year in which they turn six, and standard primary school lasts nine years, until the age of fifteen.

Secondary training and technical schools exist in Slovakia for almost every trade imaginable, and the training of young people for specific careers can begin immediately after primary school. Before entering any secondary school, however, students must apply and pass entrance examinations. If students wish to keep their options open as regards future university studies, they tend to apply to enter a secondary grammar school, or *gymnázium,* where the areas of study are mixed and more closely resemble the high schools of North Americans. *Gymnáziums* tend to be regarded as the most prestigious secondary schools in Slovakia because they give students more options for higher education, and they are often highly selective, with only the brightest students getting in.

Primary and secondary schools grade their students on a scale of 1 (best) to 5 (worst); however, compared to Western Europe and the USA, teachers tend to grant students more 1s and 2s and, as their salaries are very low, bribery is not unheard of. Although state-run educational institutions have suffered a lot from reduced funding since the fall of communism, primary and secondary education is still at a relatively high level compared to many countries in the world. The main deficiency of the Slovak education system is an overreliance on rote learning, resulting in an under-promotion of independent thought and initiative and an almost complete absence of creative thinking. On the other hand, most Slovak students know more about geography, physics, and so on than many of their North American and Western European counterparts.

Homework is generally given every day. Not many children attend after-school activities, which tend to be sports for the boys and dancing for girls (including modern forms). The after-school norm for the majority is to go out with their friends. Their parents give them pocket money. Although teens can legally start working at fifteen, there are few opportunities for paid work after school—in most regions there is not enough work for adults, let alone teenagers. The main exception to this is in Bratislava, where young people can find work in fast-food places, for example. In the near past it was unheard of for teenagers to have paid jobs outside the home—their work at home was expected to be done unpaid, and parents gave pocket money out of love, not as payment for labor.

The year leading up to graduation for a Slovak secondary school student is marked by several well entrenched rites of passage. The big event, held usually in late October or November (several months before graduation) is the *stužková*, a highly formal prom party where students host their families and teachers in grand style with food and theater. The girls go all out on their dresses, in a way that would amaze many North American and Western European women, and the boys wear tuxedos. At *stužková* each student receives a small green ribbon which they will wear prominently for the rest of the school year—a visual reminder of their forthcoming graduation. Superstition says that if you don't wear your ribbon you won't graduate. Also, in the months leading up to the *stužková*, students distribute wallet-sized graduation announcements to their friends, family, and relatives. These are artfully decorated cards featuring glamorous portraits and showing the date of the *stužková* and a list of classmates. A big class portrait is designed and produced by the students. For much of the year leading up to graduation, this is prominently displayed in the window of a shop or bank in town, and it is later put up in the school hall alongside those from previous years.

Secondary school, with all its associated traditions and rites of passage, is a time when most Slovaks form lasting friendships, which may be strengthened when members of a class stay together throughout their later studies. There are regular "class meetings" held at least every five years, and, owing to the number of vocational and professional training schools, classmates often find themselves becoming business colleagues and partners, further strengthening the bonds.

Higher Education

In their final year of secondary school studies, students usually take a school-leaving exam (*maturita*), which is the basic prerequisite for attending a college of higher education. Since 1990, however, every secondary school has prepared its own tests and questions, meaning that results are generally not comparable, so universities stage their own entrance exams. There are three types of institutes of higher learning in Slovakia: public (the vast majority of schools of higher education are of this type, financed mainly by government and sometimes business), state (military, police, and medical schools, financed by government and sometimes business), and private (established and financed by nongovernmental institutions but approved by the Ministry of Education; these are not as common as state and public institutions). As each institution of higher learning normally specializes in a particular discipline or field of study (few are multidisciplinary), universities in Slovakia are plentiful, with at least one in almost every city. Although various governments have considered the idea of charging fees for higher education, studies at state and public universities are currently free for residents of Slovakia and the EU.

University attendance, for many Slovak students, is not perceived strictly as a means of learning in and of itself. In fact, a desire to learn may be the reason for attendance for only a minority of students—most attend university because they feel it is necessary in order to acquire a particular certificate or degree to get a good job. A general lack of desire to learn for the sake of learning means that many university students admit to cheating when they feel they can get away with it, and the rote learning system of most Slovak schools means that they are neither active learners nor independent thinkers. Cheating at university in recent years has become a big topic of public discourse, with Iveta Radičová's government in September 2010 promising to pass a law to discourage academic dishonesty.

As universities in Slovakia are rarely multidisciplinary, and therefore usually quite small, there are few grand-scale campuses such as in North America or Western Europe. (University buildings can normally be spotted by pedestrians, however, because of the tradition in which members of a graduating class paint their names prominently on a sidewalk, normally in front of the university.) There is one grand exception to this rule. Mlynská dolina in Bratislava is home to ten thousand students in one town district. As one might imagine, pubs and other such establishments are plentiful here.

MILITARY SERVICE

Conscription was abolished in Slovakia in 2006, but it used to be something of a rite of passage for many young men. Between 1993 and 2005, 270,000 men were conscripted into the military, so its impact is still palpable. Nine months of mandatory military service was required of all healthy males beginning on the first day of the January following their eighteenth birthday. Exemptions were granted on the criteria of ill health, or being married and expecting a child, a single father, the only breadwinner in the family, or the only caregiver for an ill person. Alternatively military service could be avoided by working for the state (such as in a hospital, or for a municipality) for a set period of fifteen months (that is, one and a half times longer than military service). If a man was already studying at university, then conscription duties were merely delayed until after graduation.

LOVE AND SEXUALITY

Until 1990, erotic and sexual images were generally kept out of the mass media in Slovakia. Today scantily clad women and men are a common sight in advertising and the media, and there has also been a general societal shift toward more open discussions about sex and sexual morality. Schools give young people a basic knowledge of sexual anatomy and physiology, but topics such as homosexuality, sexual deviation, and sexual assault are almost ignored. As a result, children and young people tend to get most of their information on such matters from peer groups and the mass media. Attitudes toward homosexuality are predominantly hostile or ambivalent. Reported incidents of sexual delinquency are low, and sexual practices between consenting adults are not the object of legal regulation in Slovakia.

Most Slovaks' sexual relationships are based on love and partnership, and studies have shown that premarital sexual activity is common, with first sexual intercourse around the ages of seventeen and eighteen for both males and females. In Slovak criminal law, the minimum age of consent is fifteen. As in most parts of the world, heterosexual monogamy is the dominant reported pattern of sexual behavior. Incidences of "first love" resulting in marriage are common; however, studies suggest that extramarital affairs are not unusual, with between 25 and 35 percent of husbands and wives admitting to such behavior.

Since the 1990s, greater attention has been paid to sexual abuse and incest. However, a woman who reports a rape is subjected to a long and traumatic investigation by police, and a charge, once made, cannot be withdrawn. Individuals can be sued for harassment and sexually explicit language, but this rarely happens.

The general attitude toward love and sexuality in Slovakia is largely one of indifference. Both men and women can be observed in liberal, if not revealing, dress, and the subject of nudity and sexuality on display in the media is not a hot topic of debate, except perhaps among some members of the older generation. Young couples in a passionate embrace and other public displays of affection are a common sight of which most passersby take little or no notice.

THE DAILY ROUND

For some Slovaks, the day can begin as early as 4:00 a.m., particularly for people who rely on public transportation to get to their place of work. Although official business hours during the week are normally from 9:00 a.m. to 6:00 p.m. (with an hour's break at noon), many Slovaks arrive much earlier and leave later than these hours imply.

Lunch is the main meal of the day, and workplace and school cafeterias are not uncommon. Slovak labor law requires employers to provide employees with adequate nutrition in the workplace or in its vicinity. Smaller businesses and shops that cannot provide their employees with a meal give them vouchers that can be used at most restaurants, groceries, and supermarkets.

Day-to-day shopping for fresh foods is normally done by women, often after work, and not usually in large

quantities. Most Slovaks don't usually eat dinner together as a family, generally because the children and the parents come home at different times. Eating out in the evening, perhaps with colleagues or friends, is thus not uncommon, but most Slovak husbands like a hot dinner at home, and will have it at least three times a week. Dinner, Slovak-style, does not normally mean a TV dinner or a bought ready-made frozen meal. Slovak women are generally very careful about what their children eat, and many do at least some cooking every day.

Families tend to eat together only on weekends, with Sunday lunches being a common family gathering, often including the extended family and lasting much of the afternoon. Saturdays, in most Slovak homes, are days for housework. The cleaning is normally undertaken by all in the family, although mothers and daughters will still usually do much of the dirty work, such as sweeping, scrubbing, and washing.

Tepláky

As soon as she gets home from work or an errand, a Slovak woman will usually change—unless she is expecting visitors—into her *tepláky*, or "home clothes"—something informal and comfortable, like track pants and a T-shirt. While it is not uncommon for North American or Western European women to wear such clothes outside the home, the vast majority of Slovak women would never think of appearing in public dressed like this. Men, on the other hand, don't normally change their clothes on returning home, unless they wear a suit and tie to work.

This reflects the fact that Slovak women are expected to dress attractively and appear "feminine" in public, but are still responsible for the bulk of the work in the home, including the preparation of meals, tending to children, and day-to-day cleaning. *Tepláky* also speak more generally to the social importance Slovaks attach to clothes, particularly in large cities.

Women: if you are not well dressed in public, be prepared for the odd stare!

chapter **six**

TIME OUT

Slovaks work long hours, so they make sure to use their spare time well. Normally they spend their vacations and days off engaged in some kind of group activity with family or friends, very often out of doors. Visitors who have established close contacts and friendships may very well find themselves invited on such outings. And as a people who are generally quite proud of the natural wonders their country has to offer, foreign visitors can expect to get around and learn a lot on such trips. Few Slovaks will complain that they "did nothing" during their time away from work.

Heading to the shopping centers has become a hobby for many young Slovaks. With large malls springing up all over the country—particularly in West Slovakia, where salaries and employment rates are higher—consumerism is a growing pastime.

FOOD AND DRINK

Slovak cuisine, particularly in the south, shows influence from Hungary, although generally uses less paprika and spice. There is also a strong Austrian and German influence—*Wiener Schnitzel* is a Slovak favorite. The Slovak diet is generally very starchy and fatty, with a lot of meats, heavy creams, and root vegetables. It is not usual to mix salty and sweet foods, and when a foreigner is observed pairing these two, Slovaks will often comment on this with surprise.

The Slovaks are proud of their numerous natural mineral springs, and mineral waters are abundant, with many brands and different mineral contents. While North American visitors are used to "demineralized" water, Slovaks have never heard of such a process—the mineral contents of all commercially available mineral waters are listed on the labels. Plain bottled water is not always available here, but water from the faucet is safe to drink.

Until fairly recently, ordering a chilled drink at a restaurant or pub could be difficult. Even nowadays, what a Slovak considers cold and what a visitor considers cold may differ. Drinks served at room temperature are not uncommon.

Beers (*pivo*), wines (*víno*), and spirits (such as *slivovica*—the official national drink) abound. At first glance, one may think Slovak beers are surprisingly high in alcohol content; varieties are generally advertised as 11, 12, or 14 percent. But don't be fooled—this percentage refers to the density of the brew, not to the alcohol content. The higher the density, the better the quality, thus the more expensive. Most Slovak beers are the standard 5 percent alcohol content.

Invitations Out For a Meal

As with all invitations, the person issuing the invitation is expected to pay the bill. If you are a vegetarian, state this politely in advance. Few restaurants offer vegetarian dishes, and even when they do, you should read the ingredients carefully before ordering—often dishes that are listed as vegetarian include a little meat, as is often the case with the national dish, *bryndzové halušky*, which usually has a garnish of bacon.

The Slovak National Dish

Available at most restaurants, *bryndzové halušky* is a hearty meal consisting of *halušky*—small boiled dumplings, similar to gnocchi—and *bryndza*—a soft sheep's cheese. Most restaurants and households serve it with cooked smoked bacon bits and/or pork fat. Although it is widely available in places frequented by tourists, many Slovaks will tell you it is best eaten in the northern regions of Slovakia, where *bryndza* cheese was historically first produced.

If you go to a restaurant specializing in Slovak dishes, you will see that many varieties of meat and potatoes are

typical. Serving sizes will be listed in grams next to each item on the menu. English menus are not always available, and when they are can sometimes still be puzzling. Rather than pay a professional to translate their menus, many restaurants simply ask an employee, who might have taken English classes or spent a summer abroad, to do the translations. This can have some humorous results: "Mildew Breasts" for example, for chicken breasts with blue cheese, and "Giant Toothpick" for shish kebab. In recent years such translations have begun to see some improvement.

Ordered meals are not always brought at the same time. One person at your table may be served several minutes before or after the rest. Although this doesn't generally happen in good restaurants, it does in many, and nobody is expected to wait for everyone else to be served before starting to eat. But before the company tucks in, be sure to wish them "*Dobrú chut*" (literally, "Good taste"). This expression is polite, and expected.

It is considered impolite to wave a hand or snap one's fingers to attract the serving staff's attention, but the practice is not unusual. As we've seen, the quality of service can vary considerably, and sometimes waving or snapping fingers is necessary to get any service at all.

TIPPING

Tipping is not expected, and is only done in the event of excellent service. Generally 10 percent of the total bill would be considered a very healthy tip. Another rule of thumb is simply to round the bill up to the nearest €0.50 or €1.00—for example, a bill coming to €15.10 could be rounded up to €15.50, or one of €17.60 up to €18.00. The visitor who is used to leaving a tip on the table on leaving the restaurant is advised not to do so. It's usual to give it directly to the staff at the time you pay the bill.

Tipping taxi drivers, hairdressers and others is not common practice for Slovaks, but tourists are often expected to tip, so a small rounding-up may be appropriate.

Invitations Out For a Drink

Although Czech varieties are better known internationally, several Slovak beers are close—if not equal—in quality. Many Slovaks will tell you that their beer is not as good as it used to be, particularly since globalization has seen all its major brands, like Topvar, Corgoň, and Zlatý Bažant, bought up by foreign companies such as Heineken and Aegon. In days gone by, Slovak beers were a source of regional pride, with local breweries supplying the entire country. Nowadays foreign ownership has led to the relocation and centralization of breweries, and many Slovaks complain that the quality has suffered as a result, or that Czech varieties now owned by the same foreign companies are promoted over Slovak brands. Perhaps because of their long relationship with Czechs—and often being perceived as the "little sister," Slovaks often rate their own beers second to Czech varieties. Nowadays it is sometimes difficult to find Slovak beers in Slovak restaurants and pubs, in part because of the nature of foreign and consolidated ownership (this is particularly the case because restaurants and pubs normally only serve one brand of draft beer). But when inquiring as to why no Slovak beers are available on the menu, don't be surprised to hear a Slovak say "because Czech beer is better!"

Before each drink it is common to "clink glasses." When doing so, Slovaks will normally say "*Na zdravie*" ("To your health"—also said when someone sneezes) and look you firmly in the eye. Avoiding eye contact while clinking glasses is considered to be a sign of untrustworthiness, and is generally considered impolite.

Look Me In The Eye, Or Else…

If one drinking partner does not look the other in the eye when clinking glasses, the expression "*Nabudúce sa mi pozeraj do riti!*" ("Next time look me in the ass!") is not uncommon. Said with humor, it's meant as a gentle reminder of the importance of eye contact when drinking to someone's health.

There are some good wines and spirits. Particularly in western Slovakia, there are excellent varieties of wine—both commercially produced and homemade—coming mainly from the Pezinok/Modra region in the Malé Karpaty (Little Carpathian) hills. Similarly, perhaps more so in the east, you may be offered a shot or two of *slivovica*—a strong brandy (*pálenka*), often homemade, distilled from plums. Other varieties of *pálenka*, all equally strong, include *ražná* (grain spirit), *borovička* (from juniper berries), *hruškovica* (pear spirit), *jablkovica* (apple spirit), and *marhuľovica* (apricot spirit), among others.

Upon accepting an invitation out for a drink, expect to be encouraged to have more than one. One Slovak expression in relation to drinking says "one *slivovica* for one leg, another for the other leg." If you must stop, a signal that you want no more is to leave some in your glass—draining your glass dry, on the other hand, is a request for more. Serious drinking is generally understood to be more widely practiced in eastern Slovakia, but many western Slovaks can certainly hold their own. Toward the end of the night, after perhaps already too many drinks, someone may announce that the next drink is *kapurkova* ("the gate drink"). Although it is more common in eastern Slovakia, seasoned drinkers and others use this expression throughout the country. But don't be fooled; *kapurkova* is rarely, if ever, the last drink—several more are bound to follow.

If you are a nondrinker, don't feel you have to decline such invitations. Ordering tea, coffee, or Kofola, even when your host or all the other guests are drinking alcohol, is not uncommon. Teetotalers are not generally frowned upon or pressed to drink. While Slovaks may consume a lot of beer, wine, and spirits, overdrinking is not generally a problem, and public drunkenness—although seen—is no more common here than in most other countries.

Although smoking is on the decline in Slovakia, pubs and cafés can still be smoky places. In recent years nonsmoking sections have become much more common, particularly in larger establishments. Under EU regulations, businesses where food is served must now provide a nonsmoking area, or at least windows of time (for example, over lunch) when smoking is not permitted. Nonetheless, people who feel it is their right to smoke are still something of an issue. Even in designated nonsmoking areas some smokers unabashedly light up and continue puffing until staff ask them to stop. Requests from fellow customers are sometimes met with an arrogant or rude response.

PUB CULTURE

Many Slovaks spend their spare time at pubs, particularly on rainy days or in the evenings after work. Pubs are mainly, but not exclusively, frequented by men. Even young teens go to pubs for cold Kofola cola, which is served from a keg, like beer. Retired men socialize in pubs, usually in pairs or groups, and usually at establishments frequented by few others—normally the ones labeled *hostinec* or *krčma*.

Pubs and drinking establishments in general vary somewhat by type and style, depending on their clientele. Counter to what a lot of North Americans and Western Europeans might expect, pubs are not strictly places for consuming alcohol. Various types include the following.

- *Krčma* or *hostinec* generally designates a pub or tavern that also serves a limited menu or light snacks. These are more likely to be found in villages and towns, or in the industrial areas of cities. *Hostinec* were historically places where travelers stayed overnight, and were usually located close to major travel routes.
- *Bar* has essentially the same meaning as in English, and serves predominantly alcoholic beverages.
- *Vináreň* is a cellar or pub specializing in the production and/or selling of wine (*vino*).
- *Piváreň* or *pivnica* is a cellar or pub specializing in the production and/or selling of beer (*pivo*).
- *Pivovar* is a microbrewery or brewhouse, normally only where beer is produced, but sometimes also selling it.

DISCOS AND CLUBS

Discos and clubs are a hit with the young, of course, and even small towns may have one or two. Busy in the evenings—and early mornings on weekends—they are often noisy and crowded, not unlike similar establishments in other countries. Small town discos tend to cater to a very young crowd—sometimes sixteen and younger—and, like pubs, sell alcoholic and nonalcoholic beverages. The minimum age for buying alcohol or cigarettes in Slovakia is eighteen, but this is not always firmly observed or enforced.

In popular spa tourism localities, such as Trenčianske Teplice, a disco may feature live performers singing a range of pop hits in Slovak, Czech, and English, and the clientele will be normally equally split between the young and old.

MUSIC, CINEMA, AND DRAMA

Music

Music is quite pervasive in Slovak society. Popular music is generally a mix of rock, dance, rap, and folk. Music played on the radio is often a mix defying traditional genre-based programming—one minute a station will be playing Nelly Furtado or Justin Timberlake, and the next it will put on Metallica or Nickelback. Slovak-language pop groups are widespread, generally definable by the same genre categories. Czech singers and groups are also very popular—in fact, it might even be said that Slovaks make no distinction between Czech and Slovak musicians.
A Slovak group well liked across generations is the communist-era, but still active, hard rock group Élan. They and other popular Slovak groups are often appreciated as much for their lyrical content as for their rhythmic, musical, or technical abilities (for example, Richard Müller, I. M. T. Smile, or Jana Kirschner).

During the late spring and throughout the summer, Slovakia is home to numerous outdoor musical festivals, the largest of which, Pohoda, attracts performers of all musical genres, and fans from across Slovakia and abroad; the Východná festival is another huge annual event.

Despite the hostility that many Slovaks feel toward their Roma neighbors, Gypsy music is widely popular, and even celebrated as "Slovak" when its performers, such as Cigánski Diabli, find success abroad. Slovak wedding festivities often include a Gypsy band.

Rock music tends to have a healthy audience here. The continuing popularity of seasoned rock groups like Elán and Tublatanka (both of which trace their roots to the pre-1989 era) is partly classic rock nostalgia, but also partly political. Elán, for example, was closely tied to Vladimír Mečiar, the Slovak politician (generally loved by the elderly, and hated by the young) in part responsible for the splitting of Czechoslovakia. Tublatanka, on the other hand, lent their amplifiers and equipment to the organizers of the Velvet Revolution, and their song "Pravda víťazí" ("The

Truth Wins") was an anthem of that era. Although both groups remain active on the concert circuit, and are widely played on commercial radio, neither has released new material in several years.

Classical music performances are quite common in cities and towns, and classical music festivals are held in Banská Štiavnica and Bratislava. There are also popular annual jazz festivals, for example in Bratislava, Trenčín, and Nové Mesto nad Váhom.

Cinema

Going to the movies is popular as a weekend or evening activity. More people still prefer to go to the cinema than rent a DVD or download a movie from the Internet (although these are common, too). There are regular screenings of Hollywood blockbusters, which are usually subtitled in Slovak or Czech, and sometimes dubbed. Homegrown Slovak movies are becoming more common—especially those relating to Slovak history and heroes, such as *Jánošík*, released in 2009. The most popular Slovak director is Juraj Jakubisko, whose most recent work, *Báthory* (2008), was an English-language release. Hollywood releases filmed in Slovakia, with some Slovak actors, include *Dragonheart* (1996) and *The Peacemaker* (1997). Visitors who want to catch a movie should note that tickets normally designate specific seats in the cinema.

A well respected international film festival, Art Film Fest, has been held annually in the small spa town of Trenčianske Teplice since 1993. This festival screens the latest world cinema as well as significant titles in film history and audiovisual art from Slovakia. Every summer, town squares in many Slovak cities are alight in the evenings with Bažant Kinematograf, a traveling outdoor cinema screening popular Slovak and Czech movies and promoting short films by students of cinematography.

Theater

Although theaters are not as commonly attended as its Slovak advocates would like, far more Slovaks go to performances of plays, operas, and ballets than is generally the case in the USA and Canada. The theater in Slovakia is free of the class distinctions that sometimes inhibit attendance in other countries. Schools regularly take pupils to the theater as a means of promoting the performing arts. Theatrical productions are not limited to the Slovak language, but may also be given in English, for example. Theater attendance is not as high as it might be, however, in part due to the cost of tickets, but also because the content does not always appeal to younger people, who tend to go to cinemas instead.

Slovakia has both state-funded and privately operated theaters. Architecturally, many are prominent in town and city squares, such as the Slovenské národné divadlo (Slovak National Theater) in Bratislava, Štátne divadlo Košice, and Divadlo Andreja Bagara in Nitra.

SPORTS AND OUTDOOR ACTIVITIES

Football

Playing, watching, and sometimes betting on football (soccer) is a tremendously popular pastime, especially for young men and boys. Almost every city, town, and village has at least one *futbal* team, and few Slovak males are indifferent to it, as players, fans, or both. Although women tend not to play themselves, they are an element of fandom. Young women especially are enthusiastic spectators, but perhaps as much to appreciate the visual and fashionable qualities of the game—or the men who play it—as for the game itself.

The national football team's qualification for the 2010 World Cup was cause for considerable celebration (their first visit since Slovakia's independence in 1993) and the subsequent Slovak win over Italy instantly took on legendary status. Local teams, which are plentiful, also draw considerable crowds—particularly FC Spartak Trnava, ŠK Slovan Bratislava, and FC Košice. Rivalry between the fans of FC Spartak Trnava and ŠK Slovan Bratislava is often intense, and when this is combined with crowds and alcohol, the result is unfortunately often dangerous (such fans are often labeled *chuligáni*, or hooligans). Many locals avoid large congregations of football fans when important matches are at stake, so visitors, unless they consider themselves brave, or equally crazy, are advised to steer clear as well. The most notorious fans are associated with FC Spartak Trnava; Ultras Spartak, as they are known, consists of fans not only from the Trnava region, but from throughout western Slovakia, and boast the long-term highest attendance rates in the country.

Sunbathing

Particularly, but not only, for women, sunbathing during the summer months is something of a Slovak sport. Public swimming pools and lakes are often crowded with sunbathers on hot, sunny days, and some who take this activity seriously are known to arrive at their favorite tanning spot by mid-morning to get the "best sun." People also sun themselves in secluded meadows and on *panelák* balconies. Although technically not legal, topless or nude sunbathing is not a rarity—most hardened sunbathers can tell you where it is acceptable to strip off. Fair skin is a rarity here, so most people turn a nice golden brown. People don't generally worry about skin damage or overexposure to the sun in Slovakia as they do in many other countries.

Gardening

This is a major spare-time activity. For those who live in a house, the land that comes with it is most likely to be used for gardening. For apartment dwellers, owning or renting a small plot on the outskirts of the city, or in a nearby village, is very common. In both cases, these pieces of ground are almost always used exclusively for growing fruits and vegetables—if flowers are present, they are normally of types that have herbal or medicinal qualities. Gardening is not just a hobby or a means of passing the time—for many Slovaks tending a garden is something of a necessity, or at least a way of life. For many the produce is a reliable source of nourishment; for others, gardening is a routine occupation coming from the time when much of Slovakia was still rural.

Although nowadays many people living in large cities may have given up gardening due to time constraints or changing needs, almost every household either produces—or has access to, through another family member—preserves such as jams, pickled cabbage, or cucumbers, grapes for wine, or fruits such as plums, apples, or pears for stronger spirits.

Cycling

You wouldn't guess it from looking at most Slovak roads and streets—which can be downright dangerous for cyclists—cycling is a common leisure activity. There are numerous cycling routes spanning the country, and lots of informal trails too, but a recent law limits cyclists in forested areas to designated cycling routes. It's not unusual to see Slovaks taking bicycles on trains, as riding the entire distance by road is neither safe nor even possible in all cases, particularly in a short period of time.

Cycling in large cities, or as a means of generally getting around, is not as common here as in other countries, although one does see elderly people on bicycles running errands in small cities, towns, and villages.

Hiking and Skiing

As mountainous and hilly terrain is a major part of Slovakia's geography— the Carpathian arc covers almost half the country—Slovaks regularly take trips to ski in the winter and hike in the spring, summer, and fall. Renting a cottage in the vicinity of hiking or skiing facilities is popular, particularly through Christmas and New Year (although five-star hotels are available too, for those who can afford them or prefer luxury). Most Slovaks are outdoor enthusiasts to varying degrees, and many identify in particular with the mountains—the Tatra Mountains are particularly important, and are mentioned in the first line of the Slovak National Anthem. Numerous caves, castle ruins, and natural thermal springs can be found throughout the country, many of which are accessible only by hiking trails.

Some have described Slovakia as "a country full of skiers," and it's true that you would be hard-pressed to meet a Slovak who doesn't know how to ski. On most weekends between late November and the end of March the ski resorts and slopes are crowded. Although only three slopes rise above around 4,900 feet (1,500 m), most resorts offer wellness centers and massage services. The Tatras are the obvious choice for skiing, but there are smaller slopes on other ranges too.

A very popular region for hiking is Slovenský Raj (Slovak Paradise), a national park in the central-eastern part of the country. Numerous hiking trails, of a variety of lengths and levels of difficulty, are the main draw here, and the adventurous hiker (weather permitting) will be rewarded with breathtaking views of valleys, canyons, gorges, waterfalls, and a number of plant and animal species. The Malé Karpaty (Little Carpathians) region in the southwest is another area offering a variety of hiking possibilities—but hiking trails are common throughout the country.

Gathering Mushrooms and Herbs

A widely practiced spring, summer, and fall activity for Slovaks of all ages is picking mushrooms. Due in large part to family tradition—and school instruction in some cases—many Slovaks are adept at identifying the edible varieties, although the odd incidence of poisoning is not unheard of. Several towns have offices, usually offered by the local health authorities, where mushroom consultants are available to inspect and advise on unfamiliar varieties. Particularly in October, after a heavy rainfall, entire families will get up very early in the morning and venture into the forests to collect the night's crop of mushrooms, which are either cooked for that day's lunch or dinner or dried or marinated for later consumption.

Many people also go out to find and pick various herbs, mainly because herbal remedies are cheaper than the over-the-counter varieties. For example, in spring, villagers harvest elderflowers. These white, sweet-smelling flowers are combined with water and sugar to make syrup that is bottled and used to ease stomach pains and to sweeten tea. Nettles, dried and used to make tea, are also known to have a soothing effect on the stomach.

Other Recreational Activities

Many Slovaks love to swim, and with indoor pools and various aquatic centers located in the larger towns and cities

across the country, this activity is not exclusive to the summer months. The Danube's shoreline on the Petržalka side of Bratislava is transformed every summer into a makeshift beach, where among other activities (with the notable exception of swimming), beach volleyball competitions are held.

Finding a decent tennis court in Slovakia is not difficult, as the game is much played, both recreationally and competitively, by young and old. Other popular activities are horseback riding, rollerblading, fishing, rafting, and mountain climbing. Golf—until recently only associated with Americans for most Slovaks—is becoming more common among the business class.

Spectator Sports

The main spectator sports, in addition to football, include ice hockey and tennis. The Slovak men's national hockey team is among the top national teams in the world, and regularly competes in international championships. Since 1993, the men's national hockey team has won three medals in World Championships, including a gold medal in 2002.

The 2011 World Championships were held in Bratislava and Košice. In Olympic competition, Slovakia's best achievement so far has been fourth place (in Vancouver in 2010). At least seventy Slovak players have played in the National Hockey League (NHL) including Peter Šťastný (1980–95; Quebec Nordiques, New Jersey Devils, St. Louis Blues), Marián Gáborík (2000–present; Minnesota Wild, NY Rangers), and Jaroslav Halák (2007–present, Montreal Canadiens, St. Louis Blues), to mention only a few. The small city of Trenčin (pop. 56,760) can boast that it has produced per capita the most NHL players in the world. The Slovak *Extraliga*, the highest-level hockey league in the country, consisting of thirteen teams, is one of the strongest leagues in Europe. Women's hockey, however, is not well developed or widely appreciated. At the international level, the women's national team has competed at several World Championships (with no better than a tenth-place finish) and one Olympic Games (in 2010, finishing in eighth place).

Where women thrive on the Slovak sports scene is in tennis, where they are an impressive force on the international stage. Top-ranked professional women in the sport include Dominika Cibulková, Daniela Hantuchová, and Magdaléna Rybárikova, among several other past and rising stars. The well-known Swiss player Martina Hingis was born in Košice and began playing tennis in Slovakia. Slovak male players who have been a force on the world stage include Dominik Hrbatý and Karol Beck.

VACATIONS

As we have seen, Slovaks are hard workers, often putting in long hours—sometimes at jobs they care little for—out of financial necessity. However, when it comes to vacations, most people make the most of their time off. Workers are entitled to a minimum of twenty paid days of vacation per year; after the age of thirty-three, this rises to twenty-five paid days of vacation.

Most Slovaks take their vacations in June, July, or August, or around Christmas time—in other words, in their children's school vacations. These are busy times of year on the roads, the trains, and at the airport.

Within Slovakia, popular vacation spots include Slovenský Raj (mainly for hiking), the Tatra Mountains (for a range of activities, from hiking and skiing to simply relaxing at a cottage), natural spa towns (which are abundant and serve a range of purposes, from merely relaxing to medical treatments), and aqua parks (which in recent years have sprung up all over the country).

Outside Slovakia, popular holiday destinations include Croatia, Greece, Italy, Egypt, Spain, and Lake Balaton in Hungary. Some university students take advantage of summer work and travel programs in the USA and Canada. Slovakia's membership in the EU has in recent years resulted in some university students working within Europe too during their summer vacations.

chapter **seven**

TRAVEL, HEALTH, & SAFETY

Slovakia's stock as a travel destination has deservedly risen in recent years—despite the less than flattering representations in Hollywood movies such as *Hostel* and *Eurotrip*. Lying in the center of continental Europe, it is easily accessible by train, plane, car, and even boat (cruises on the Danube between Vienna, Bratislava, and Budapest are frequent) and traveling within the country is relatively easy and efficient.

As regards the social side of travel, Slovaks are not known for their chattiness, at least as far as striking up conversations with strangers goes. However, some will carry on conversations at maximum volume (face-to-face and on cell phones) on crowded trains and buses, as though no one else were there, although many consider this impolite.

ARRIVAL BY AIR

The largest and generally most convenient airport (in terms of flights available and costs), through which most visitors to Slovakia travel, is Vienna's Schwechat International Airport, some thirty-seven miles (60 km) from Bratislava. Vienna's airport is larger than Bratislava's International Airport, M. R. Štefánik. Slovak taxis are available at Schwechat, with fares starting at €66. Austrian taxis can be much more expensive. But by far the best way to travel between Bratislava and Schwechat is by bus—several run per day. The fare is around €14, and the journey takes between an hour and an hour and a half, depending on the traffic.

Bratislava's M. R. Štefánik International Airport is five miles (8 km) from the center. Taking a taxi from here should cost between €7 and €14. City bus number 61, which takes you to the main railway station, is also an option. Bus tickets—at €0.60 each—are purchased from a yellow ticket dispenser before entering the bus, and must be validated in the red punch machine after boarding. If you have large luggage, a €0.35 ticket for each piece should be purchased.

If you are arriving in eastern Slovakia, your likely entry point will be Košice International Airport, four miles (6 km) from the center. The Košice airport offers limited flights to Vienna, London, Dublin, Poprad, and Bratislava.

TRAINS, BUSES, AND TRAMS

Slovak bus and train services are very good. So good, in fact, that car ownership is not nearly as widespread as it is in North America or Western Europe. Many Slovaks do not own cars, but rely on buses and trains to get them anywhere they need to go, whether it's a major city or a small village.

Fares are reasonable compared to costs in the USA or Western Europe.

Traveling by train is the cheapest and most reliable means of getting around. The official Web site of the national railway company, www.zsr.sk, provides scheduling and cost information. Tickets can be purchased at stations, at windows labeled KVC (*Komplexné vybavenie cestujúcich*). Fast trains (*rýchlik*) and slow trains (*osobný*) —which stop at every station—are available. Trains can be very crowded during the summer, on weekends, and if there's a special event such as a summer music festival. Under such circumstances it can be virtually impossible to secure a seat in second class (many will be left standing) unless you purchase a seat reservation (*miestenka*), which at other times is not necessary. First-class cars are rarely crowded, but although they cost more, they are not dramatically different in terms of comfort or service. Slovak trains have improved in recent years, but many old wagons that are still in service lack any means of temperature control—except to open or close the window—and can sometimes be smelly and noisy.

If you are traveling as far as Žilina, or further east, the best way is to take a train labeled IC or EC. These are a little more expensive, but they are newer, faster, and cleaner, with better onboard service, and stops are announced in English. Reservations are mandatory.

When traveling by bus within the country, tickets must be purchased from the driver as you board. During busy periods like Christmas, drivers sell tickets to as many people as they can fit on the bus—standing passengers pay the same price as those with a seat, so consider buying a reservation from the ticket office in the bus station (*autobusová stanica*) if it is a state bus (operated by the state) or try online for private bus companies like Slovak Lines, Euro Lines, Žltý Expres, Student Agency, or

Turancar. You could also arrive early and get a place in line. As with trains, bus station stops are rarely announced, so unaccustomed travelers will have to keep a sharp eye out for their desired destination.

Some bus terminals and train stations have seen a number of aesthetic improvements in recent years, but still many major stops, such as Bratislava hlavná stanica (main station), Trnava, Banská Bystrica, and Košice, leave much to be desired. As the entry point for many foreign travelers, Bratislava's main station is particularly in need of a major makeover.

Most, if not all, major cities and towns have public transportation services in the form of buses, and in some cases trolleybuses and/or trams. The Slovak expression for city bus is *autobusy*, trolleybus is *trolejbusy*, and trams are known as *električky*.

Ticket costs vary from town to town but are normally quite reasonable. Schedules are posted at each stop, although they may not be easy to decipher (as can be the case with countrywide bus service schedules). Škoda-made trolleybuses are a common sight in Bratislava, Prešov, Banská Bystrica, Košice, and Žilina, and trams are present in Bratislava and Košice. The Web site www.imhd.sk provides information and schedules for all urban public transport in the country.

TAXIS

Taking a taxi, even in Bratislava, used to be cheap by Western standards. But with the adoption of the euro, this has changed and fares have dramatically risen. Dishonest taxi drivers unfortunately do exist, particularly at the main railway and bus stations in Bratislava, and foreigners are obvious targets. Make sure the meter is set before starting on the journey, or you may otherwise find yourself faced with an outrageous total.

Taxi drivers do not generally have broad language skills, so communicating in English can be a problem. Clearly writing your destination (in Slovak, of course, if possible), or presenting a business or calling card with an address may be helpful where verbal communication is impossible.

Calling a taxi by phone is cheaper than hailing one on the street. Note that the dispatcher will normally tell you what kind of car to watch for, and its registration number, to deter a competing driver listening in on the same radio frequency from attempting to steal the fare.

RENTING A CAR AND DRIVING

Renting a car in Slovakia is not normally difficult. The Internet is perhaps the best resource in terms of price comparison and availability, as there are many companies offering rental services, but calling and booking at least a week in advance is recommended. Rental companies should not charge extra for things such as highway permits, but be careful to ascertain whether or not your fee includes a limited number of kilometers.

Driving in Slovakia is not for the timid. Depending on your experience, it can be a considerable challenge. Slovak drivers are notoriously aggressive, with few observing speed limits or even basic rules of courtesy.

SPEED LIMITS

In cities, the speed limit is 50 kmph (31 mph) unless otherwise posted; on highways the limit is 90 kmph (56 mph); on freeways it is 130 kmph (80 mph). The speed limit at railway crossings is 30 kmph (18 mph). These limits are generally not posted.

The last several years have seen an expansion of freeways, but there are fewer the farther one travels from Bratislava. Two-lane roads are thus often crowded in peak tourist seasons with big, slow, exhaust-spewing trucks, old Škodas, and speeding BMWs. Be prepared to yield to oncoming vehicles that have moved over into your lane to pass. Also keep an eye out for cyclists, who often try to share the main roads despite very narrow or nonexistent shoulders. Cycling, as we have seen, is a popular activity for Slovaks, but many roads are rather dangerous for both cyclist and motorist.

Certain sections of freeways and some highways require a motorway permit sticker, which must be displayed on the right-hand side of the windshield. Unattached stickers are considered invalid. Annual, one-month, and seven-day stickers can be purchased at most gas stations.

Foreign drivers with valid national driver's licenses should also consider obtaining an international driving permit, which in theory is recognized by Slovak traffic authorities.

TRAFFIC REGULATIONS

These are the broadly the same as in other European countries, but there are certain points to keep in mind.

- The use of cell phones while driving is forbidden.
- No turning right on a red light.
- Streetcars turning right have the right of way.
- There is a zero-tolerance rule regarding alcohol and driving. Not even one beer or glass of wine is acceptable before driving; and if you've had a lot to drink the night before, you may need to reconsider driving in the morning. Passengers are not restricted from drinking alcohol in cars. As long as the driver has had none, open bottles of alcohol are permitted.
- All auto accidents with damages greater than €3,000 and/or injuries must be reported to the police. In cases where damages are small, and no one is injured, only insurance companies need be called.

Foreign drivers are strongly encouraged to buy the best road map possible—one featuring even small villages and secondary roads, as the smallest places may be important road marks. This is particularly relevant for travel in Middle Slovakia, where because of the terrain there may be only one route to your destination. Slovak drivers tend to think of roads and highways in terms of the nearest or largest city or town rather than route numbers, meaning that when asking for directions one is likely not to be told the route number (such as "E77") but to turn left or right, or "direction Banská Bystrica," for example.

The most common car by far in Slovakia is the Škoda. Once firmly associated with communist Czechoslovakia,

Škodas are today produced by Volkswagen in the Czech Republic and are a reliable, affordable, and fashionable choice. Older models are still a common sight (affectionately called *Škodovka*), although their number declined dramatically after 2008, when the Slovak government introduced an initiative to support the automotive industry by offering €3,000 toward a new vehicle when trading in an old model. As Slovakia is home to major manufacturing plants for Kia Motors, Peugeot, and Volkswagen, these makes and models are also a common sight on the roads. The vast majority of cars in Slovakia are standard transmission, so bear this in mind when considering rental. Fuel prices, as is the case in much of Europe, are generally more expensive than North American drivers are used to.

Škoda!

In a rather strange linguistic quirk, the word *škoda* translates into English as "it's a pity" or "damage." The manufacturer, however, takes its name from the family name of Emil Škoda (1839–1900), the Czech engineer and industrialist who established Škoda Works in 1869.

Traffic reports are broadcast on most Slovak radio stations, particularly Rádio Expres. Some visitors are surprised at the legal reporting on radio of the location of speed traps. Slovak police generally use an unmarked car to gauge the speed of fellow motorists; when speeding is detected, the car will radio ahead to other officers who will pull the offending driver over. Radio stations regularly report the location as well as the color, make, and model of the undercover car, as a warning to drivers. Oncoming motorists also often flash their headlights to warn other drivers of the presence of police ahead—a gesture that most Slovak drivers return, in thanks.

Being pulled over by the police used often to involve officers asking motorists to pay "fines" in cash on the spot. Of course, receipts were not issued, and the practice was, and is, illegal. It is thankfully on the decline these days, and it is anyway rare for foreign drivers to be asked to pay cash on the spot—if only because Slovak police are not known for their foreign language abilities—but such questionable police activity goes a long way to explaining the distrust and cynicism many Slovaks feel toward law enforcement.

WALKING

Slovaks are avid walkers. Walking, even among the elderly, is perhaps the most common means of getting around and doing daily errands, particularly in towns. And, as we have seen, recreational walking in good weather, and on weekends, is a popular activity. Many of the old castles and other ruins found throughout the country are accessible only on foot. Hiking trails are

generally well indicated with signs and marked trees, but not necessarily well maintained, so the experience can be rather rustic—and, unfortunately, often littered with garbage.

Walking in most cities or towns, on the other hand, is often made difficult by old and poorly maintained sidewalks; many are badly cracked, buckled, and bubbled. Like a lot of the infrastructure, they were built during the communist era, when aesthetics were not considered important. Bad sidewalks require one always to keep an eye on the ground, or risk tripping or twisting an ankle. Some sidewalks are now slowly being repaired.

When crossing the street in towns take care to use, and in using, the crosswalks (*zebra*) and traffic signals for pedestrians. Slovaks drive fast and aggressively, and will not usually stop for a pedestrian who is waiting to cross the street. Aggressive walkers—who step into crosswalks without looking or pausing to check whether approaching traffic is stopping—should not automatically expect cars to stop, and accidents involving Slovak drivers and naive foreign pedestrians are not unheard of. According to the law, a driver should stop for a pedestrian in a crosswalk, but most Slovak drivers interpret this as merely a suggestion, and you are advised to wait until the way is clear before attempting to cross.

CYCLING

Potential cyclists need to remember that Slovak drivers are very aggressive, and that riding a bicycle on the roads can be dangerous. A recent law stipulates that cyclists outside urban areas must wear a reflective safety vest and helmet—a sensible precaution considering the absence of shoulders on most Slovak roads. Cycling in wooded areas is forbidden except on recognized trails.

CHANGING MONEY

Slovakia adopted the euro (€) on January 1, 2009, so changing money if coming from other parts of Europe may not be necessary. But if you do need to change currencies, do not—under any circumstances—exchange money in the street with strangers offering this. They are most likely to be thieves who will undersell you, give you worthless bills, or just run away with your money. Look for offices labeled "change" or "*zmenáreň*."

Perhaps the easiest and safest means of getting cash is from an automatic teller machine (*bankomat*), most of which will work with international bank accounts. Travelers' checks may be cashed at most banks and some exchange offices, and credit cards—although not universally accepted—are commonly accepted in cities and sites accustomed to tourists.

WHERE TO STAY

Where to stay while visiting Slovakia largely depends on what you want to do. With all kinds of accommodation to

choose from, ranging from bare-bones cottages to five-star hotels, it really comes down to your budget, preferences, and means of travel. Bratislava, of course, is the most expensive city in which to stay, but it boasts the greatest variety in terms of location, cost, and service. Several Internet sites offer information and services in terms of bookings, but generally the most efficient means of inquiring about or reserving a room is to call. Hotel staff in the popular tourist areas speak various languages.

Booking your accommodation before arriving in Slovakia is recommended but not essential. Hotel, hostel, and *penzión* proprietors will not normally be seen at bus and train stations advertising rooms to let, as in some adjoining countries, and tourist information booths are present only on occasion at the Bratislava train station and airport.

The most common form of accommodation—and usually the most comfortable and affordable—is a *penzión*—a boarding house, or guesthouse. This is normally a family-owned establishment with only a few rooms. By law, rooms must have a private bathroom, and breakfast is often included. Full and half board may also be arranged at some *penzióny*.

Hotels in Slovakia are normally given star ratings, and unless labeled as *garni* will have full or half board available at an adjoining restaurant. *Garni* hotels offer breakfast only.

In spa towns or areas with recreational facilities (such as hiking trails, skiing, and so on) there is normally an additional fee of approximately €0.50 per adult guest per night added to your bill. This goes to the town to cover the costs of infrastructure and maintenance of the recreational facilities.

HEALTH

The Slovak health care system is generally good, although almost every Slovak has a horror story to tell about poor medical service, long waiting times, illogical bureaucracy, or unfriendly doctors, nurses, and hospital staff. There is a government-subsidized public medical system, which means that medical care is free (for Slovaks), with the exception of dentistry. In this system you can pay a fee, perfectly legally, to jump to the head of the line. There is also a private system, in which patients pay and expect shorter waiting times and better care.

Public medical professionals are generally very poorly paid in Slovakia, and hospitals themselves sometimes look very shabby. The lack of money partially explains the less than friendly service and long waiting times that many Slovaks complain about in the public health care system. But compared to service and waiting times in some public health care systems elsewhere—say Canada, for example—the Slovak system is not really so bad. The quality of medical service itself is good. For patients who can afford it, making a gift (in the form of cash or good alcohol, for example) to one's doctor is not unusual, and such practice is considered normal. For the very rich, waiting times and service can be dramatically improved.

SAFETY

Slovakia is generally safe, or is at least no more dangerous than many other modern countries. Nonetheless, tourists should be on their guard against pickpockets in crowded places and the usual scams aimed at foreigners. Many Slovaks point to the Roma population as the perpetrators, but criminal behavior can come from anywhere. Slovaks will also talk about the local mafia (known to be involved in murder and car bombing, for example), who can generally be identified by their expensive black cars and clothing. Many wealthy Slovaks, in fact, will avoid buying black cars, for fear they will be incorrectly associated with the mafia. However, mafia crime is not normally directed at tourists or foreigners, except in some (probably shady) business situations.

Acts of violent crime are uncommon. The highly publicized story in 2010 of a gunman killing seven—including six members of a family who were specifically targeted—and injuring fifteen in the Bratislava suburb of Devínska Nová Ves was a highly unusual and tragic event. This shooting spree, which had no precedent in Slovakia (except for mob-related violence in the 1990s), has resulted in stricter controls on gun ownership.

chapter **eight**

BUSINESS BRIEFING

Slovak identity, tradition, and modesty are the three most important things to consider when doing business here. We have seen that the Slovak people have a long history and a strong sense of identity. Take care, for example, not to confuse Slovakia with Slovenia, as some people do (most famously, former US President George W. Bush and Italian Prime Minister Silvio Berlusconi), or assume that there is no difference between Slovakia and the Czech Republic. Remember that traditions influencing gender relations, notions of hierarchy, and forms of address are important, as is the fact that quiet modesty is valued over brash self-confidence.

Overwhelmingly, Slovak business culture is based on personal relationships. However, legal regulations exist outlining the rights and obligations of employers and employees. These are administered by the Slovak Ministry of Labor, Social Affairs and the Family, and all foreign businesses looking to establish themselves in Slovakia should take note of the Slovak Labor Code and the Act of Employment Services.

Reflecting the central importance of friendships and family in Slovak culture, in many business situations Slovaks will normally first network with their families, friends, and personal contacts who may owe them a favor, rather than go through official channels to get something done. However, granting privileges to people purely on this basis is generally avoided, being regarded as unethical.

Without articulating it explicitly, Slovaks practice a kind of balanced or symmetrical reciprocity in their exchanges with others. What this means is that one good turn deserves another; when someone does something beneficial to someone else, there is an unarticulated expectation of a fair return at some undefined future date. This is based on trust and social consequences—that is, someone who accepts gifts or favors without ever giving in return will find it harder to obtain similar favors in future. However, if you are offered a gift, it is customary to refuse the gift initially, and on the second or third offer to accept it.

A CHANGING ECONOMY

As we have seen, the Slovak economy is still in a process of transition. Although the Velvet Revolution was more than twenty years ago, transformation from a centrally planned to a market-driven economy is not complete, and still presents challenges. Some forms of behavior and business practice are holdovers from the communist era, but, regardless of these, many business-minded Slovaks are forward thinking and eager to develop the country's economy and encourage foreign business investment.

SETTING UP A MEETING

Office hours are normally between 9:00 a.m. and 6:00 p.m. Remember that many people take their vacation in the summer, and some businesses close for weeks in July and

August. Business visitors are likewise advised to take note of Slovak public holidays (see page 69).

Appointments should be arranged in advance. Punctuality is important, so avoid being late for meetings, and stick to deadlines. Slovaks take time seriously, and showing respect for this is not only polite but demonstrates good intent.

There may be linguistic difficulties. If you make an appointment by telephone, it is advisable to send a confirming e-mail, letter, or fax. Ask what language your Slovak colleagues prefer as regards written documents and contracts. Offering to bring an interpreter to meetings may be a good idea—just be sure to arrange such things well in advance.

Although English is the predominant business language in Slovakia, and most educated Slovaks understand it (although to varying degrees), providing information in Slovak will normally be seen as a gesture of seriousness and goodwill. The use of written summaries and notes may be helpful in minimizing misunderstandings.

As a general rule, it is better to be formally dressed than dressed down or casual. Although the dress code largely depends on one's position and where one works, a business suit is appropriate for managers and executives, while lower-ranking employees may look slightly more casual. Women won't go wrong with a business dress or a skirt, jacket, and blouse.

INTRODUCTIONS AND GETTING STARTED

The senior person present will usually set the agenda and conduct the meeting. Developing good personal relationships and establishing respect and credibility are of primary importance in doing business with Slovaks. On meeting—whether for the first or the hundredth time—shaking hands is the most accepted form of greeting. However, it is polite for a man to wait for a woman to extend her hand first. Also remember that formal and professional titles should be used when greeting or addressing business colleagues. The North American practice of starting off on a first-name basis is not well received. First names may be used once people know each other better, but the visitor should wait for the suggestion.

COMMON SLOVAK ACADEMIC TITLES

Ing. (*Inžinier*) Engineer
Ing. arch. (*Inžinier-architekt*) Engineer of Architecture
MUDr. (*Doktor medicíny*) Doctor of Medicine
MVDr. (*Doktor veterinárnej medicíny*) Doctor of Veterinary Medicine
Mgr.art (*Magister umenia*) Master of Fine Arts
Mgr. (*Magister*) Master
Ph.D. or **ArtD.** Doctor of Philosophy or Arts
JUDr. (*Právník*) Lawyer

Maintaining eye contact with your business partner is an important part of communicating, and indicates that you are serious and trustworthy. Avoiding eye contact may make people doubt your sincerity. Maintain an arm's length distance when speaking. In business situations touching another person is uncommon, and even considered unacceptable.

Business and professional relationships are normally established over meals and often bonded and sealed with alcohol. Small talk and exchanging personal experiences with your Slovak business partners is recommended before getting down to the matter at hand. But be warned—the weather, politics, and money should generally be avoided as these topics are regarded as boring and only mentioned when people do not know what else to talk about. Establishing your credibility through an appropriate—if not delicate—balance of modesty, seriousness, and personal rapport is essential.

Once friendship and trust have been gained and established, the job is essentially half done, but such relationships naturally take time, and weeks or months may be needed to achieve your object. One-off business visits of a day or even a few days are normally of limited value. There is a strong preference on the Slovak side for dealing with the same person or persons throughout a business project, so it is advisable to maintain this continuity. In small-scale projects, most Slovak companies tend to prefer dealing with smaller firms where responsibility lies with the top executive, rather than being spread over many people.

PRESENTATIONS

The Slovak communication style is normally characterized as direct, yet diplomatic, with sensitive information being delivered in a subtle manner. But due in large part to the communist system—where there was no reason to present and sell your products—Slovaks are generally not very good at presentations and selling themselves. Basic presentation skills are for the most part undervalued and neglected, even in the education system. It is not unusual, for example, for presenters educated exclusively in Slovakia to begin their talks by outlining the weaknesses of their product or project. This has a lot to do with the Slovak tendency to be modest. Therefore aggressive, know-it-all-style presentations are not generally appreciated or effective.

When attending a presentation, Slovaks will often interrupt to ask questions or make comments, rather than waiting until the end. This is especially true of existing clients. If they are prospective clients and no questions are forthcoming, don't assume lack of interest—they may be too shy to break the ice. Humor and patience are helpful here—as long as the jokes are not directed at them, of course. Attention wanes after about forty-five minutes in most cases.

NEGOTIATIONS

In most cases, the client will decide what language is to be used in the negotiation process. If you use an interpreter, be sure it is someone with whom you have a good relationship.

In negotiating prices there are two predominant attitudes. Large companies tend to try to get the price down as far as possible, exerting their influence as the stronger party; in this situation contractors may in the end provide a low-quality service. Other Slovak businesspeople may prefer to negotiate a reasonable (not necessarily the lowest) price, but demand good service.

Be sure to make all prices and costs quite clear in advance. Some firms tend to "forget," and add costs as the project progresses, thus charging more in the long run than they'd originally quoted. Sometimes the other party will suggest leaving some details open, but attempt to clear these up as soon as possible. Although certainly not every Slovak businessperson will try to take advantage of loose ends, the practice is not unheard of.

Navigate the negotiation stage with care and formality. Humor is not appropriate here—you may be thought disrespectful or suspect. Later, once it is quite clear that both parties are satisfied, you can be a little more relaxed.

When business is conducted between two private persons, or between a private person as a client and a company, negotiations relating to price will often be done in person, rather than by e-mail or post.

CONTRACTS

As contracts and work agreements vary on a case-to-case basis, generalization is difficult, but some basic characteristics normally apply.

Slovaks generally prefer handshakes and gentleman's agreements over formal contracts. However, one should never enter into business with an unknown party without a contract, except perhaps in a situation where only a small sum is at stake.

Slovakia has a civil law system based on Austro-Hungarian codes, complying with the obligations of the Organization on Security and Cooperation in Europe (OSCD). It is not normally necessary to employ lawyers to handle a contract, but it is up to the parties to decide. Because of the expense involved, lawyers are sometimes deemed too costly for a small project.

In Slovakia the renegotiation of contracts is not unusual, but this should be done carefully and according to the rules established in the original contract. Trying to renegotiate a contract without a reasonable argument will certainly risk your credibility, so ensure that renegotiation is really worth it.

Although Slovaks appreciate punctuality on the part of their foreign business partners, when it comes to deadlines make sure that your Slovak counterpart understands how important it is to complete the project on time. Throughout the project it is worth politely contacting your contractor several times in order to confirm that everything is being done on schedule. If you don't do this, he may get the impression that the ultimate deadline is not important. In dealing with companies you have not worked with before, a clause in the contract indicating late fees is not a bad idea.

Employment contracts are mandatory in Slovakia. These are based on a written contract between the employer and employee, and may be concluded for a fixed or indefinite period. Fixed-period employment contracts may be agreed to for up to three years, and within this time may be extended or renewed once. In cases where work is taken on outside an employment relationship, a work agreement must be drawn up.

MANAGING DISAGREEMENTS

Disagreements, in the vast majority of cases, are dealt with personally rather than resorting to the law, thus personal relationships remain important. The main reason for this lies in the fact that when a party does decide to sue, the process can take a long time—five to ten years in some cases. Also, the quality of law enforcement in

Slovakia, especially as regards business, is generally quite low, and there is very little trust in the court system due to high levels of corruption and alleged ties to the mafia (particularly under the governments of Mečiar and Fico).

There is a top-down management tradition in many Slovak businesses, so employees are not normally accustomed to expressing their ideas and opinions to those of higher rank, and generally expect to receive and carry out instructions. They are not used to questioning or disobeying superiors. However, there will always be a minority of employees who do question their superiors, or even ignore management requests.

Most Slovaks have a strong sense of personal pride. When conflicts or problems arise, these should be dealt with privately, or within a close group of colleagues. Closely related to this, Slovaks are normally hesitant to criticize foreigners, and in their own business relations problems are often dealt with on an ad hoc basis, and sometimes even ignored until they become critical.

Foreigners at the helm of both small and large companies in Slovakia are not unusual, and their success is due in large part to their ability to adapt to local business and practices. If they respect Slovak manners and business culture while only gently introducing new ideas and philosophies, then employees tend to respond positively.

SOCIALIZING AND WORK

As personal relations form the basis of business and working relationships, these often give rise to friendship and socializing away from work. Most Slovaks count at least some colleagues as friends too, and due to the nature of their high school and university education, many are also former classmates. In small firms bosses are sometimes invited to social outings after work, for example. Maintaining positive relations, as much as possible, through regular greetings and friendly body language, is an important aspect of Slovak society generally, but this is especially the case in work relationships.

Coworkers often travel and stay together on work-related retreats or courses, both within Slovakia and abroad. Such trips, often combined with recreational activities, tend to reinforce social relations. Celebrating name days and birthdays with colleagues is also common. Usually such events will take place in the workplace, after normal work hours, or in a local restaurant or pub.

chapter nine

COMMUNICATING

At once open, direct, and hospitable, the Slovaks are generally good communicators. However, not all have a good grasp of the English language, and sometimes their style may seem abrupt, unceremonious, and even rude. Rarely, if ever, will you encounter someone in the public sphere who is flowery or unnecessarily wordy—Slovaks waste little time in making themselves understood. A waiter, for example, will never use small talk in an effort to appear more personable, as is the case in other countries. But in their personal relations, Slovaks are friendly and outgoing, and few topics of conversation are considered out of bounds.

When friends and acquaintances meet, whether they are two women or a man and a woman, they double kiss—on the right side first. Men generally shake hands warmly. It is important, when shaking hands, to remove your glove. Former US President George Bush failed to do so upon meeting the Slovak president and prime minister in 2005, and the Slovak media were quick to criticize this.

LANGUAGE

The Slovak language is officially separate and distinct from Czech, but the two tongues are quite similar; they are distinguished by differing grammatical structures. Like Czech, Slovak is part of the Slavic subgroup of languages, which also includes Polish, Russian, Ukrainian, Belarusian, Bulgarian, and Serbo-Croatian.

Slovak employs a variation of the Latin alphabet, with diacritical marks above some letters. Over some consonants one will find a *mäkčeň*, or "little hook." For example, *s* is pronounced in the same way as the English "s," but *š* is pronounced as the English "sh" (as in "shape"). The letter *z* in Slovak sounds like the English "z," but, with a *mäkčeň, ž* sounds like the English equivalent of "zh." Another diacritic, the *dĺžeň*, indicates the length of the sound. A *dĺžeň* can appear over any vowel and indicates that it should be voiced longer than an unmarked vowel (for example: *á*, *é*, *í*). Slovaks tend to be particular about spelling and grammar, and mistakes in English by English speakers are usually seen as a sign of poor intelligence.

The vast majority of Slovaks have no problem whatsoever understanding Czech. Even young people born after the Velvet Divorce feel comfortable communicating in Czech. Young Czechs, however, often have difficulty with Slovak. One of the main reasons for this imbalance is that Czech programs dominate Slovak TV—this is particularly true with regard to children's programs—and Czech movies are much more common in cinemas than Slovak ones. In large part this is simply due to economics—with a much larger population, and thus a larger audience, Czech TV and film production is better funded. Foreign TV programs and films are also often dubbed or subtitled in Czech, rather than Slovak, for similar economic reasons. Children's programs, the vast majority of which are produced outside Slovakia (or the Czech Republic), are thus always dubbed in Czech, and thus Slovak children are exposed to it very early. As cable channels now broadcast all-day children's programs, many young Slovaks are more exposed to Czech than their parents were, even though the parents were probably born in Czechoslovakia.

Ahoj!

"*Ahoj*" (pronounced ah-HOY or AH-hoy), the most usual informal greeting between Slovaks, has been in popular use only since the 1960s. Used when people meet and when they part, the word first entered Central Europe with the English phrase "Ship ahoy!" through German literature in the early nineteenth century. By the end of that century it was associated mainly with rowing clubs, and was borrowed by outdoor groups in Bohemia in the early twentieth century. "*Ahoj*" entered the media and mass culture in Czechoslovakia in the 1930s, gradually replacing "*Servus*" as an informal greeting by the 1960s. Since the 1990s, the use of "*Čau*" has slowly been gaining currency.

A General Lack of English Where it Counts

It is often a source of frustration to foreigners that few Slovaks in bureaucratic service positions, or in the service industry, seem to have a working knowledge of English. Thus, even dealing with the immigration or foreigners' police departments, or bank tellers, for example, can be a challenge (although even native Slovak speakers will tell you that it's not easy to deal with the "bureaucrats behind windows," who apparently operate in their own language and with their own logic). This is particularly true of those over forty. Young people who have been educated since 1989 have a far better grasp of English. If you have a problem, seek out a young person, and the chances are that they will be able to help.

Recent government measures to make the instruction of English mandatory in schools, beginning in the third grade, may help to improve this situation in future. However, the availability, not to mention the quality, of such instruction is in question. Teachers' low salaries don't generally attract top-notch professionals with teaching or language skills, and judging by comparison with other European countries, native-speaking English teachers are also discouraged by the low pay—most teach in private schools, where they generally earn a higher salary.

Some Slovak Proverbs

Kto druhému jamu kope, sám do nej padá.
He who digs a hole for another falls in himself.

Hovoriť je striebro, mlčať zlato.
To speak is silver, to keep quiet is gold.

Ryba a návšteva smrdí rovnako po troch dňoch.
Fish and guests both smell after three days.

Although Slovak is the official language of the Slovak Republic, knowledge of German, Hungarian, Russian, or Polish, in addition to English, would be helpful. Slovaks educated before the fall of communism learned Russian, and German is the second-most common language of business after English. As another Slavic language and a neighboring state, Polish is generally understandable to most Slovaks, and a sizeable Hungarian-speaking minority lives in southern Slovakia. Before the Second World War, most members of upper-class Bratislava society spoke Slovak, German, and Hungarian, and possibly other languages as well.

PHYSICAL SPACE AND CONTACT

When standing in line at a supermarket or waiting to board a bus, visitors to Slovakia will observe that Slovaks pay little heed to other people's sense of personal space, crowding in to the point of touching, in some cases. Westerners allowing what they perceive to be a polite space between themselves and the person ahead may lose their places, as from a Slovak point of view that's empty space waiting to be filled. This is in part explained by the recent political past in Central Europe, and by the close quarters in which many Slovaks live. With hundreds of people living in a small apartment block, a Slovak's sense of privacy and personal space is understandably different, and during the worst times of communist rule some foodstuffs and other products were hard to come by. Thus mild jostling to get what one needed was not uncommon.

HUMOR

Slovak humor consists almost entirely of jokes, satire, parodies, and irony. Practical jokes or pranks (referred to inexplicably as *Kanadské vtipy,* "Canadian jokes") are not generally appreciated. For the most part, Slovaks don't laugh at or make fun of other people—unless, of course, the other person is a foreigner attempting to speak Slovak, which often results in smiles and laughter.

Kremnické Gagy, an annual festival of humor and satire, has been held in the Middle Slovak town of Kremnica every summer since 1981. Popular elements of this festival include an improvisation competition and the awarding of Golden Gander prizes by the Slovak Academy of Humor in several categories. Kremnica is also home to the Alley of Famous Noses (Ulička slávnych nosov), a permanent exhibition of face sculptures commemorating Slovak artists who inspired joy, hilarity, and good humor in their times.

Homegrown sitcoms, such as *MafStory*, and *Susedia* (*Neighbors*) are well-known lowbrow TV programs, as are several American sitcoms—dubbed into Slovak or Czech—such as *The Cosby Show*, *Friends*, *Frasier*, and *The*

Simpsons. Sedem, s.r.o. and *Show Milana Markoviča* are two popular, more highbrow programs combining news parody and satirical editorial. Stand-up comedy is a relatively new form for Slovaks that has gained some popularity in Bratislava, but not so much elsewhere.

Have You Heard the One About . . . ?

Why does a Škoda come equipped with a rear-window defroster? So the driver can keep his or her hands warm while pushing it.
How do you double the value of your Škoda? Fill the tank with gas.
What do you call a Škoda convertible? A dumpster.
What do you call a Škoda driver who says he or she got a speeding ticket? A dreamer.

* * *

What is the difference between an Englishman, a Frenchman, a Jewish man, and a Slovak man?
An Englishman has a wife and a lover, and he loves his wife.
A Frenchman has a wife and a lover, and he loves his lover.
A Jewish man has a wife and a lover, and he loves his mother.
A Slovak man has a wife and a lover, and he loves his drink.

* * *

A tourist comes to a shepherd's hut in Orava (in north-central Slovakia) and asks: "Shepherd, do you know where *slivovica* is distilled here?" The shepherd looks toward the village in the valley and replies, "Do you see the church?" "Of course," says the tourist. "So, except for the church, everywhere."

THE MEDIA

Since the end of 1989, the Slovak media has slowly been transformed from restrictive state-controlled institutions to a more or less dual system of public state media and private independent publications and broadcasting organizations. After the fall of communism and the breakup of Czechoslovakia, a number of private broadcasters, newspapers, and magazines were launched in Slovakia, but freedom of the press has not been universally enjoyed. Particularly between 1992 and 1998, an oppressive environment was instigated by the government of the day in which state-run media outlets were bullied into pro-government coverage. Even nowadays, as recently as the Fico administration (2006–10), accusations of government influence in the media have been made. The country's literacy rate (those over the age of fifteen who can read and write) is 99.6 percent.

Most Slovak households nowadays have cable TV (UPC Communications Ireland Limited is the largest cable provider in Slovakia), so there are a number of national and international channels from which to choose. In terms of Slovak TV programming, there is one state-owned broadcaster—Slovak Television (Slovenská Televízia)—which broadcasts on three channels: Jednotka ("One"), Dvojka ("Two"), and Trojka ("Three"), an all-sports channel. There are several commercial companies, including, Markíza, TV JOJ, and TA3 (all-news), and each city normally has its own local station with local programming.

There are several weekly and daily newspapers, the best-known of which are *SME*, *Pravda*, and *Nový Čas*. *The Slovak Spectator* (est. 1995), a weekly now published by *SME*, is the only English-language newspaper in Slovakia. The highest-selling daily is *Nový Čas* ("The New Times"), a tabloid, with a circulation of around 200,000. Two-thirds of the Slovak population below the age of forty-five read this daily, with women making up more than half of its readership. *SME* is Slovakia's second-most widely read and perhaps most influential daily. Established in 1993, *SME* was a vocal opponent of the governments of Vladimír Mečiar and is more or less a center-right-wing newspaper. *Pravda* ("Truth"), which was once the official paper of the Communist Party of Slovakia, is today still one of the country's main newspapers, with a mainly older readership.

Popular commercial radio stations include FUN Rádio and Rádio Expres—their content is for the most part music and entertainment, with only a minimum of news programming. Slovenský rozhlas (Slovak Radio) is the national public-service radio broadcaster, which currently broadcasts six radio channels and two digitally broadcast channels. Radio Slovakia International (RSI) is the country's official international radio broadcasting service, with programs in English, French, German, Russian, and Spanish.

MAIL

Main post offices (*Slovenská pošta*) are normally open Monday to Friday, 6:00 a.m. to 6:00 p.m., except over the lunch hour, and Saturdays from 6:00 a.m. to 12:00 midday. Post offices are multifunctional institutions. In addition to handling mail, they double as places to buy phone cards, make calls (using pay phones), pay bills, develop film, buy lottery tickets, send money abroad, and send telegrams. You wait in different lines for these various services. To send a letter, look for a position labeled *odosielanie listov* or *listová prepážka*.

Sending a parcel abroad normally involves using a separate window (sometimes a different room or separate entrance) labeled *balíková prepážka*. Parcels should be wrapped in plain paper, with one side clear of tape so the address is fully visible, and bound with string. The contents and their value must be entered on a form provided by the post office. For an extra sum you can bring an unwrapped item to the post office, where it can be wrapped and bound for you.

TELEPHONE AND INTERNET

Cell phones are ubiquitous in Slovakia. Many people have two, sometimes even three—one for each provider (Orange, T-Mobile, and O2). SMS, or text messaging, is generally cheaper than calling and is very common, particularly with the young.

Landline telephones are increasingly rare, as calls between landlines and cell phones are quite expensive. Most pay phones in Slovakia are card operated. Phone cards (*telefónna karta*) may be bought at newsstands, gas stations, and post offices. International calling cards will also work in most cases.

USEFUL TELEPHONE NUMBERS

General Emergency (police, ambulance, fire) 112

Emergency Road Service 18124

Directory Information 1181

According to statistics issued by the International Telecommunications Union in 2010, 74.3 percent of the Slovak population are Internet users—a percentage that has almost doubled since 2006. This rise is in part due to a Slovak government program called *Infovek* that has provided funds to equip every elementary and secondary school with high-quality Internet access and develop digital literacy. As almost every Slovak home now has Internet access, and large cities now host Wi-Fi zones (as do some buses and trains on major routes), finding an Internet café is becoming increasingly difficult outside major tourist areas.

The main Internet service provider is T-Com, resulting from the 2010 merger of T-Mobile and Slovak Telekom; other main ISPs include Orange Slovensko, Chello, and Wimax. These providers offer a range of connections and are available in almost every town. The Slovak Internet country code is .sk.

CONCLUSION

As we have seen, Slovakia is a young country with a long history, an enduring culture, an old language, and a people who are quietly proud and modestly optimistic. The country's recent history has been one of frequent change, but the traditions of the Slovak people are rich and easily perceived in the architecture and geography of their surroundings, in their customs and celebrations, and in their general warmth and determination.

Although Slovakia is small, it has much to offer, and the Slovaks are generally hospitable, and proud to show their country to the curious guest. Visitors who dare to step outside Bratislava's Staré mesto (Old Town) and move away from the crowds of tourists will be rewarded both in human terms and by the varied natural and built landscapes that lie beyond. And for those visitors who don't have the time to explore what lies outside the capital, it is hoped that your experience will also be enriched by what you've read in this book.

Armed with the basic information provided here, combined with an open mind and sensitivity to difference, your experience in Slovakia will be memorable. Of course, the country is much more than what has been described in the preceding pages, but every effort has been made to capture the essence of what makes Slovakia unique. Take the time to get to know this modest, stoical, humorous, and responsive people, and no matter where your journey in Slovakia takes you, you are bound to warm to them, and to leave yearning to return. And although every journey includes inevitable obstacles and occasional frustrations, it is what we learn from these that ultimately makes travel so worthwhile and rewarding. *Ahojte*! *Dovidenia*!

Further Reading

Bán, Andrej. *The Other Slovakia: Photographs 1989–2005*. Bratislava: Slovart, 2005.

Cravens, Craig. *Culture and Customs of the Czech Republic and Slovakia*. Culture and Customs of Europe Series. Santa Barbara: Greenwood Publishing Group, 2006.

Dvořák, Pavel. *Pictoria: The early history of Slovakia in images*. Photographs by Jakub Dvořák. Budmerice: Rak Publishing House, 2006.

Henderson, Karen. *Slovakia: The escape from invisibility*. Postcommunist States and Nations Series. London: Routledge, 2002.

Hurn, Margarete. *The Foreigner's Guide to Living in Slovakia*, version 1.2. San Diego: Modra Publishing, 2007.

Kirschbaum, Stanislav J. *A History of Slovakia: The struggle for survival*, 2nd revised edition. New York: Palgrave, 2006.

Kollár, Daniel, Ján Lacika, and Peter Podolák. *Slovakia: Travelling around regions*. Bratislava: Dajama, 2003.

Leikert, Jozef and Alexander Vojcek. *55 Loveliest Places in Slovakia*. Bratislava: Priroda, 2007.

Škvarna, Dušan, et. al. *Slovak History: Chronology & lexicon*. Trans. by David P. Daniel. Bratislava: Bolchazy-Carducci, 2002.

Spectacular Slovakia 2010, 15th edition. Bratislava: The Rock, s.r.o., 2010. (Published annually by *The Slovak Spectator* since 2005; written by a different native English speaking journalist each year.)

Online Reading

www.slovakia.travel
Slovakia: little big country. (Official Slovak tourism Web site)

www.fgslovakia.com
The Foreigner's Guide to Slovakia. (Web site and blog supporting the independently published book by Margarete Hurn)

www.spectator.sme.sk
The Slovak Spectator. Bratislava: The Rock, s.r.o. (Web site of the only English newspaper in Slovakia)

Index

Acknowledgments

The author is very grateful to the following friends who helped tremendously in offering insight, explanation, and ideas: Tatiana Bachárová, Lenka Bubanová, RNDr. Mária Glasnáková, Iveta Kovacová, Mgr. Veronika Králíková, Ing.Arch. Miroslav Marko, M.Arch., Gina Medairy, Ph.Dr. Emília Mironovová, Lucia Otrísalová, Ph.D., Veronika Patalášová, and Dana Prasilová. The students and fellow teachers at Canadian Summer School 2010 in Trenčianske Teplice were also invaluable in terms of offering ideas, advice, and support. A particular debt is owed to Veve and her roommates in Trnava for their generous hospitality and patience.

The final outcome of this book has benefited a great deal from the advice of Slovak, expatriate, and visiting friends, but any errors, oversights, or unintentional misrepresentations are entirely the responsibility of the author.